SEE ME
HEAR ME
KNOW ME

The Heart of A Caregiver

EVELYN JOHNSON-TAYLOR, Ph.D., RN
CONTRIBUTING AUTHOR: SCOTT B. TAYLOR

See Me Hear Me Know Me

See Me Hear Me Know Me – *The Heart of a Caregiver*

Copyright © 2017 Evelyn Johnson-Taylor and Scott B. Taylor

All rights reserved. No part of this publication may be reproduced, stored in a retrieval system, or transmitted in any form or by any means, electronic, mechanical, digital, photocopy, recording, or any other except for brief quotation in printed reviews, without the prior permission of the publisher.

Unless otherwise indicated, all Scripture quotations are taken from THE HOLY BIBLE, NEW INTERNATIONAL VERSION®, NIV® Copyright © 1973, 1978, 1984, 2011 by Biblica, Inc.™ Used by permission of Zondervan. All rights reserved worldwide. www.zondervan.com. Scriptures marked KJV are taken from the King James Version of the Bible. The KJV is public domain in the United States.

Please note that Promise Publishing House will capitalize all pronouns that refer to the Father, Son, and Holy Spirit. Note that the name satan and related names are not capitalized. We choose not to give him the same acknowledgement, even to the point of violating the rules of grammar.

Published by:

PROMISE PUBLISHING HOUSE
PO Box 46753, Tampa FL 33646 | www.promisepublishinghouse.com

FIRST EDITION

Library of Congress Control Number: 2016921555

Written by: Evelyn Johnson-Taylor and Scott B. Taylor

Cover and Formatting by: Eli Blyden

ISBN: 978-0-9908338-4-0

eBook ISBN: 978-0-9908338-5-7

Journal ISBN: 978-0-9908338-6-4

Category: Motivational/Inspirational/Christian

For Worldwide Distribution

Printed in the U.S. A.

Dedication

This book is dedicated to
my husband Scott B. Taylor

Thank you for teaching me
more than I ever thought I could learn about
For Better or for Worse
In Sickness and in Health

And thank you for your contribution to
this important message.

See Me Hear Me Know Me

Thank You

Thank you to our family, friends, and my brothers and sisters in Christ. Many of you have stood with our family and supported us over the years from near and far. Whether you visited, cooked a meal, sent a card, made a call, or said a prayer. Thank you for being there, it is in the dark moments that true love brings needed light. May God continue to bless each of you for all that you have done to assist us during Scott's illness. I am convinced that without your love and support, I would never have made it this far.

See Me Hear Me Know Me

Table of Contents

Dedication III
Thank You V
Special Acknowledgement IX
Preface XI
Introduction XIII
My Prayer for Caregivers XXIII

TWO HEARTS JOINED AS ONE
Our Story 3
The Diagnosis 9
Stem Cell Transplant 15
Cancer or No Cancer 25

EMOTIONAL ROLLERCOASTER
Caregiver's Grieving Heart 31
Heart of Contentment 39
Heart of Faith 53
Forgiving Heart 63
Heart to Do Good 73
Hopeful Heart 81
Kind and Loving Heart 89
Lonely Heart 105
Heart of Patience 117
Peaceful Heart 125

Quiet My Heart 131
Thankful Heart 137

I SEE YOU, I HEAR YOU, I KNOW YOU
Heart of the Patient... 147
Epilogue 153
Resources and References 159

Special Acknowledgement

Amanda F. Bond

~

D'Athlone Brown

~

Anita Lawrence

~

Robin Jamison

~

Tyrone Johnson

See Me Hear Me Know Me

Preface

Our lives were completely altered when the telephone rang. The doctor's assistant's voice said, "You need to see an oncologist," only minutes before their office was about to close. It was a completely unexpected turn of events. How does an appointment for testing of back pain lead to an oncology consult? And how could the doctor send such a message with no explanation? That telephone conversation sent us on a quest redefining our roles as husband and wife. As a result of the journey we were about to embark on, I became a caregiver for my forty-eight-year-old husband.

Caring for a loved one is most likely one of the greatest challenges a person can face in life. Many have walked this road before me and offered insight, and for that I am grateful. Each person's journey is unique, but the mission remains the same. How do you care for a loved one in a way that adds value to their life while not diminishing the value of your own life?

When I use the term caregiver, I am referring to an unpaid individual who is involved in assisting others with activities of daily living and/or medical tasks. It has been said that the caregiver must first take care of themselves before they can adequately take care of another. While I agree with this statement wholeheartedly, it is not always an easy thing to do. How do you manage to schedule and maintain your own health with routine checkups when your loved one has frequent medical appointments? How do you get proper exercise when your loved one needs your seemingly constant attention? How do you enjoy a good meal when your loved one does not want to eat what you cook? How do you give yourself the evening off or take a day for yourself when you have no one to fill in for you? Taking care of yourself as a caregiver is not always an easy task, but it must be a priority if you are to survive the road ahead.

I was blessed to assist in the care of my father for a few months before he transitioned from his earthly to eternal home. My mother was in the home, and frequent visitors including other family members would stop in. There was life and joy in their home. Doctor's appointments were minimal, and eventually he was admitted to hospice. I remember the environment being one of tranquility. My experience of caregiving for my father was radically different from where I found myself seventeen years later becoming a caregiver for my spouse.

Introduction

Since June 2008, I have been my husband's caregiver, and it has not been an easy task. While his complaints have varied over the years, my role of caregiver has been constant. The level of care he has needed has changed, sometimes more or less, but I have remained his caregiver.

Emotionally conflicted daily, this has been one of the most perplexing journeys of my life. This experience has been confusing and frustrating, but it has also been gratifying to know that God has given me the grace to minister in this capacity.

Though I am a registered nurse by profession and worked in the field of nursing for more than fifteen years, I was not prepared for the voyage I was about to embark on as my husband's caregiver. Nor did I anticipate how it would alter our marriage. Once a spouse becomes a caregiver, the marriage is different. The changes are not always negative, and some couples grow closer during an illness. However, the relationship is altered nonetheless.

My husband's illness shifted our relationship but not in the way we would have chosen. I think partly because of the nature of his illness we experienced many conflicts. He would go through periods of independence where he needed little or no help but like a ticking time bomb, we never knew when this would change. He literally goes from walking with a cane one day to not getting out of bed the next day. In fact as I write this, he is still in bed and it is well past noon. The uncertainty of his condition has infused great disruption into our marriage.

He has been hospitalized multiple times. This includes being placed in intensive care, acute care settings, rehabilitation centers, and outpatient therapy. His journey has included chemotherapy, a stem cell transplant, surgery, outpatient infusion centers, doctors' appointments, and home health therapy, some of which continues even today.

Thanksgiving, birthdays, Valentine's Day, Christmas Eve, and other special days were spent in a hospital at his bedside. I remember visiting him on Valentine's Day while he was inpatient preparing for his stem cell transplant. It became our routine to expect the unexpected making it difficult to make any special plans.

Over the years, we became remarkably familiar with the staff at several of the local Tampa hospitals. At one time or another we have spent time in most of them. We went through an array of specialists and physicians looking for answers, including multiple visits to the Mayo Clinic in Jacksonville, Florida. Contacts were made for the Mayo Clinic in Minnesota, Cleveland Clinic and John's Hopkins. Never wanting to settle, you keep searching, hoping, believing, trusting, and living. Maybe just maybe the next doctor will say something that brings relief and change. The only thing we both really wanted was for life to be "normal" again. We desired the life we once had where we planned vacations, special events and holidays. But we finally came to the realization that this was now our story and we had to accept it. He is ill and I am his caregiver. Our new roles had been defined, and we needed to adjust our dreams, hopes, and expectations.

Although I am still in the middle of my journey as a caregiver, it is my wish to inspire others. It is my hope that others who are in the role of a caregiver will experience encouragement while reading *See Me Hear Me Know Me.*

Introduction

The smile on the face of the caregiver does not show what she or he is going through. In the middle of caring for a loved one, the caregiver may be experiencing great emotional pain. However, the caregiver may feel that they should not complain because they are not the one who is ill, not wanting to seem self-absorbed, they keep their feelings to themselves.

It is important to realize that the caregiver's story still has value. While the pain of the caregiver may not be physical like that of the patient, the pain of the caregiver is real and valid. The different emotions and challenges that they face can be devastating and frustrating. Because the caregiver looks physically healthy, people ask, "How is the patient?" They rarely question how the caregiver is faring. In some cases, the caregiver may feel like the invisible victim. All the concerns are for the patient as the physical struggles of the patient overshadow the needs of the caregiver. As long as the caregiver is functioning, everyone thinks that he or she is all right.

Caring for a loved one is a tough assignment, especially when a woman is caring for her husband. There are many men who take their responsibilities seriously as head of their family, and they want to be able to provide for their families. This is not simply limited to earning money for their wives and children, but men also desire to be able to contribute in such simple ways as helping drive on a long trip or completing home improvement projects. When they are unable to do so, they feel they are failing to live up to their role as a man. This is especially true of godly men. In my own life, I have seen this with my husband. The fact that he needs a caregiver has been extremely difficult for him. His illness has not only impacted his physical health but also his mental self-worth. Having his self-worth damaged has been especially hard for me. Being a caregiver means recognizing that physical illness comes with mental struggles as well.

Fulfilling the emotional care component of my role of a caregiver has not been easy for me. And even more complicated for me has been my ability to not do irreversible damage to my own value as a human being and as his wife in the process of emotionally supporting him. When a person is ill, there is a selfish element that is visible. If the caregiving spouse is constantly giving out accolades or affirmation and receiving nothing in return, she or he will soon become depleted. Everything that you learn about asking for what you want in a relationship does not work when your spouse is ill. My husband's illness and pain level being so high has made it hard for him to focus on anything other than the pain. Thankfully, prior to his illness he was a person who gave compliments freely and often, so I would need to pull from my storehouse of tributes and be satisfied for the moment.

Just as challenging can be a husband caring for his wife. Generally, the woman by nature is a nurturer. Her intrinsic instinct is to care for others. Many women take care of their families, including their husbands, for many years. As household manager, she shops, plans, and cooks the meals. She leads the day-to-day operations of the home and family and is comfortable carrying out that role.

When the husband must assume the role of caregiver for his wife, being the nurturer becomes a new chore he must learn. He often has limited experience in being a caregiver. This role does not come as naturally to him, and it can be difficult to take on.

Most caregivers go about their daily task not asking for accolades or awards. They perform their duties out of love and compassion for the person for whom they care. Despite the demands and frustrations that accompany caregiving, many still consider it an honor and a blessing to care for the people they love.

In sharing my thoughts and feelings over the past years as a caregiver, I want to encourage others. Whatever you may be feeling

Introduction

is valid. The load gets heavy at times, and there have been days when I felt like going for a long walk and never coming back. The pressure can be overwhelming and the feelings of being alone are unbearable at times.

Caregivers, you are not alone. Others have walked this journey before you and have survived. Countless others will come after you and need your encouragement to make it through their journey. Our circumstances are diverse but our goals are identical. Caring in a way that portrays love and commitment to those we love.

Feelings of happiness and discontent simultaneously are not unusual for me. Even in my darkest moments and when my emotions are fragile, my faith in God sustains me. My journey has not been without its trials, mistakes, and deficiencies, but I have gained a considerable amount of wisdom and insight along the way regarding what it means to care for a person who is struggling and in a place of dependency.

As a special bonus, my husband has brought awareness from the patient's perspective. As a contributing author, he shares briefly his views on what the patient needs from the caregiver. He truly wanted to contribute to this project, and I welcomed his input.

For you to fully understand our journey I share a brief synopsis of our background story; the road to how we got to the place we are today: How we met and how our roles were altered in this season of our lives. Our story is not that different from others who have suffered major illness, but when you are in the middle of life's challenges, you sometimes feel like you are the only one. I never dreamed I would be a caregiver to my forty-eight-year-old husband. The longevity of it all has taken its toll on our relationship and on our lives in general. I share candidly about the challenges I have faced as a believer. We were a ministry couple, pastors on Kingdom assignment and life happened. Our lives took an unexpected turn and even today several years later, I wonder, *How did this happen?*

I admonish all to see, hear, and know the heart of the caregiver. Do not just look at the task they perform but see the heart they use to perform the task. Caregivers are real people with real emotions ranging from one end of the spectrum to the other. Many times they're afraid to express their feelings for fear that others will think they are insensitive.

No caregiver wants to say out loud that, "I am angry, hurt, lonely, or disappointed." You may not be able to verbalize the words, but God sees your heart. He knows the pain and the struggle that caregivers face. Caregiving may be one of the most difficult jobs you will ever do in life. In many cases, the pain of the caregiver is equal if not greater than the one who is ill. See the caregiver, hear the caregiver, and get to know the caregiver.

What started out for me as a short-term caregiving assignment has seemly turned into a lifetime assignment. We are entering our ninth year of the journey and it has not been easy. It has changed our lives in ways that we never envisioned. Our finances have been tapped at a level that only God would restore.

Both of our girls have graduated from college. Our youngest daughter is currently enrolled in a doctoral program. The oldest one finished her graduate work and has joined the professional workforce. My husband has had to take a back seat to many of the highlights of their lives, his illness has caused him to miss some of their milestone moments. Sickness has kept him from attending some events, but we have done our best to accommodate him as much as possible. Life does go on even in the midst of disappointment and tests. I am thankful that in the middle of it all that our girls still have their father.

Because of the unpredictable behavior of his disease, I am unable to seek full-time employment. I continue to write books, speak, and

Introduction

travel when I can. I have experienced doubt, faith, hope, sadness, joy, discouragement, fear, and many other emotions in one form or another. Over the years my energy has declined leading to bouts of depression, frustration, and at times hopelessness. I have experienced some sleepless nights wondering how we were going to make it, but here we are nearly nine years later and life continues. Maybe not the way we wanted, but each day brings with it new challenges and new hope.

I could not begin to tell you how we made it, but I know it was God who kept us. I want to share with you some of the things I have dealt with along the way and hope it will be beneficial to anyone in the position of caregiver to a loved one.

What started as a brief interruption in our lives turned into a major life-altering shift. My husband now battles an autoimmune disease which affects his central nervous system. No physician has authenticated my theory, but I believe that after the stem cell transplant his immune system did not recover correctly causing an autoimmune disorder.

He is now permanently disabled and requires a caregiver. Some days are better than others and he continues to strive to do things for himself. The first year with the cancer treatment and the recovery from the stem cell transplant had its challenges, but those were different from the challenges we now face.

He has experienced great frustration in dealing with the pain and not being able to do the things he once enjoyed. He has experienced major life changes and I sometimes marvel at the fact he is still standing, figuratively speaking. Honestly, I do not know if I could have endured everything he has been through. I often refer to him as the strongest man I know.

It is a constant challenge to educate healthcare personnel when he is hospitalized because this disease is rare and few have heard of it. It can be frustrating for both he and the staff as they try to meet his needs. I have spent many late nights and early mornings in the hospital just to act as an advocate for him. At times, I would spend the night to ensure that I would not miss the doctors who make rounds at five-thirty in the morning.

In the chapters of this book, I will deal with my thought processes, emotions and some of the challenges I have faced. I will share honestly some of my struggles as a caregiver. At some of my most desperate moments I have not been able to find words to describe how I felt. It has been the grace of God that has kept me standing. In those moments where I lack patience and it seems easier to turn and walk away, I thank God for His grace.

I have had to apologize when my actions have not demonstrated endurance. It is easy to love and be patient with someone when things are going well, but true love shows up when things are not.

I challenge any single woman who desires to be married. Be sure you marry a man you truly love. Do not only love what he does or what he has but love who he is today and who he might become tomorrow. Life will never prepare you for the kind of shake up a major illness brings into a marriage. When I stood before the pastor over twenty-five years ago and said, "With the help of God I will," I had no idea of what was down the road for us. When we say for better or worse, we are generally thinking about the better. And when we say for richer or poorer, in sickness and in health, we are thinking riches and health. I can honestly tell you that without the help of God there is no way I could have made it during these difficult years.

When I vowed before God and the people to love my husband, being his caregiver for nearly nine years was not what I had in mind. When a couple dreams of marriage and the life they will build together, they are usually thinking of great achievement: having children, purchasing a home, and building an exciting life together. I have heard

Introduction

some say that what they learned in the struggle they would not trade for anything. Well, I am not there yet. I would gladly trade this life for the one I had imagined.

Our faith has been tested, and the struggle to maintain contentment and peace is real for me as his caregiver. There are times when I feel isolated, not because I do not have people in my life. But I feel isolated because I do not know how to express my needs in words that people will understand, as often I do not understand myself.

I chose to write this book now while I am still caring for my husband. Many times after an event is over, we tend to glamorize it only remembering the good parts. Sharing my journey while it is still fresh in my mind allows me to share an authentic view of my experiences and lessons learned.

One thing I have learned is that a thankful heart brings joy like a medicine. As you read this book, I pray it will encourage you on your caregiver's journey to stay the course as you care for your loved one. Remember the loved one you care for is not only loved by you but also loved by God. This book is a testimony of the goodness of God as I could not write it any other way. I recognize that without God I would have never made it this far.

This book includes a resource/reference section to further assist the caregiver. There is also an accompanying journal with thought-provoking questions for you to record your thoughts after you read each chapter.

See Me Hear Me Know Me

My Prayer for Caregivers

Heavenly Father,

I pray now for the reader of this book. It is my desire that the caregivers who reads this book will understand that You are with them. Let them know that they are not alone and that You will restore them day by day. I pray that You will surround them with people who can be there to support, love, and assist in whatever needs to be done. Help them to realize that even when they make mistakes, Your loving hand is there to guide and direct.

Remind them, God, I pray that the loved one that they care for is not just their parent, child, or their spouse, but that person is also Your child. And just as You love the caregiver, You love the one that they care for.

Dear Father, many times the road is rough, and the mountain is hard to climb, but we know that You are able to assist us on this journey. Give the caregiver Your peace that passes human understanding and help those of us who care for loved ones to trust You more. Even in those times of hopelessness, may we be reminded that our hope is in You.

Thank You, Father, for the time You have given me through the pages of this book to share and encourage those who care for loved ones. I pray that You will help us as caregivers to show love and compassion as we care for the people we love. The task of caregiving is difficult and sometimes seems impossible to accomplish, but God we thank You for being there to accompany us on the journey. Thank You for your Spirit that abides in all who love and trust You. Help the caregivers to rest in Your loving embrace.

Your Word says that You will never leave us, and we trust Your Word. You are a present help in the time of trouble. According to Your Word in Psalm 34:19, "The righteous person may have many troubles, but the LORD delivers him from them all." God, we trust You for deliverance out of whatever situation we may find ourselves in as we care for our loved one.

I ask Your blessing upon us and the ones we care for this day. Thank You for hearing our prayer. I thank You for each person who will be encouraged by this book. May this book fall into the hands of those who need it most. Even as I have written and remembered, I have been blessed so I pray that the pages of this book be a blessing to others.

In Jesus' name, Amen.

TWO HEARTS JOINED AS ONE

See Me Hear Me Know Me

Our Story

"'For this reason a man will leave his father and mother and be united to his wife, and the two will become one flesh.' So they are no longer two, but one flesh. Therefore what God has joined together, let no one separate" (Mark 10:7-9).

On June 1, 1991, we stood before God and about three hundred guest and said, "I will with the help of God." We were introduced by a family member and we communicated by telephone several times before meeting each other in person.

At the time of the first telephone call I was in North Carolina assisting my mother with the care of my father. I had taken a leave from my job at Capitol Hill Hospital in Washington, D.C. as a registered nurse to be a caregiver for my father who had been diagnosed with cancer. My mother was unable to care for him alone, and at the time my family and I decided that with my nursing experience I would be the one to assist her. It seemed like a good time for me to take leave, and it was a good way for me to use the education my parents paid for by assisting them in their time of need. My father required lifting and turning, and I was more than happy to fill this role at this time in my life. I ran errands to and from the pharmacy, gave him medications, cooked, cleaned, etc.

The first call from my future husband Scott came rather unexpectedly as I was focusing on the assignment at hand, caring for my father. After the first conversation, he called me each day, and it was nice to have a temporary diversion. When he tells the story, he leaves out the part that in our first conversation he shared with me that he was looking for a wife.

I too had prayed and asked God for a husband, but at this season of my life I was not focusing on that. My life had taken quite a radical turn in the matter of a few weeks. I sold my home in Maryland and went to live with my parents. At the time, I was planning to relocate closer to home so I could help my parents. But in the process of job hunting, my father's condition grew worse, and I decided to take a leave of absence and put my plans on hold.

The hospital where I was employed offered me an opportunity to work a few shifts a month and maintain part-time employment. Since I had multiple family members in the area that I could stay with, it was decided that I would come back once a month and work two shifts. The first time I returned to Washington, D.C. for my two shifts in intensive care, I received a call. It was about lunchtime and I was on the first day of my work commitment. My father's hospice nurse called to let me know that my father's condition had taken a turn for the worst.

I left work immediately to return to my sister's house to collect my things and travel back to North Carolina. Just as we were getting on the highway, I got a call from my brother that our father had passed away. At the time, it did not make sense that I would relocate to North Carolina to assist in his care only to be away at the time of his death. I had left my home in Maryland to be there for this season in his life. I went from sleeping in my large bedroom in a king-size bed to sleeping in a bunk bed in the bedroom across from where my father slept at night. The location of this room made it easy for me to hear him if he needed anything during the night. I would get up throughout the night to turn him from side to side to prevent his skin from breaking down. After all the lifestyle changes I had made, it was beyond my understanding why God would take him while I was away. It was not meant for me to be there on his last night and later I understood why. My time with him toward the end of his life was extremely rewarding and I still look back on it with no regrets.

The few months I was in North Carolina with my father before he passed was when Scott and I connected. I met him face-to-face for the first time on my trip back to Maryland to work at the hospital. A friend was getting married that weekend, so I scheduled to work while I was there for the wedding and would meet Scott at the same time. The same weekend I met my husband, God called my father home.

Before Scott and I met in person, he would call me daily and we would talk for hours on the phone. I was up most nights anyway, taking care of my father so his calls were a welcome distraction. At the end of each conversation, we would pray together on the phone.

In one of our early conversations, maybe the first one, he told me about his primary years and some health challenges he had as a child. He shared with me that he had rheumatic fever while in middle school, and at the age of seventeen he was diagnosed with Hodgkin's lymphoma, cancer of part of the lymphatic system affecting the lymph nodes.

He discussed with me that he had received radiation therapy for the cancer and was deemed cancer-free after treatment. Because I was a nurse, I think he felt comfortable sharing about his previous health issues.

He had a close relationship with his mother as he was an ill child and often missed school. He would have tutors which allowed him to keep up with his school work. Other than his illness, his childhood seemed magical. His mother would make every holiday special for the family and as a result, he loves decorating and celebrating holidays. His face still lights up when he speaks of his years growing up in upstate New York.

After my father passed, I returned to Maryland to resume the life I had left behind, only this time, I was engaged to be married. Scott had asked me to marry him over the phone and gave me a ring the first time we met. I truly believe the hand of God was at work. I had accomplished what I had gone to North Carolina to do and now I could move forward.

Scott and I spent as much time together as possible getting to know each other. He was exactly the kind of man that I had asked God for. I asked for a man that loved Him more than he loved me. I knew that if he loved God enough, that would mean he would love me the way God said that he should.

My experience affirmed to me that God's plans for us are not always the plans we have for ourselves. He brought me right back to the place I had left. I found it interesting that in all my time in Maryland I had never met Scott. My nephew introduced us after I left Maryland.

After our wedding, we experienced seventeen years of married life without any major health concerns, had two daughters and all seemed well. He worked; I stayed home with the girls. My days were spent in the parks, taking long walks, visiting with other moms, and performing other mommy duties. Scott would come home in the evenings and everyone would be super excited to see him.

We were both serving as leaders in our local church. Scott was on the ministerial staff and I served as a lay leader. About two years after our marriage, Scott felt God calling him to start a ministry. So we were not only the parents of young children but pastors of a young ministry. Our lives were filled and extremely busy.

Our Story

We served the people God had given us while he continued to work a secular job each day. I worked part-time one evening a week and Saturdays while Scott was with the girls. We went on a family vacation each year, usually to Disney, and life was good. A thought of his cancer returning was not something that ever entered my mind. And never did I think I would end up as his caregiver at such a young age. After all, I had been caregiver for my father and how often does the same person get to be a caregiver more than once in one lifetime?

See Me Hear Me Know Me

The Diagnosis

"They will have no fear of bad news; their hearts are steadfast, trusting in the LORD" (Psalm 112:7).

While doing a practice exercise at the martial arts studios where he trained frequently, Scott sustained a back injury. His physician ordered a magnetic resonance imaging (MRI) of his spine because he was complaining of back pain after the fall. This test would allow the physician to see if he had sustained any injuries to his spine and recommend any necessary treatment. The MRI revealed a herniated disc and an incidental finding of an enlarged lymph node in his abdomen area.

After a battery of tests and biopsies including a bone marrow biopsy, it was determined that he had Stage IV Hodgkin's lymphoma. The staging is determined based on whether or not the cancer has spread to others parts of the body. The bone marrow biopsy confirmed that the cancer had indeed spread to other areas of the body. His spleen on exam showed enlargement. The physicians were in disbelief that he had not experienced any night sweats, weakness or weight loss. This diagnosis took us all by surprise. How could Hodgkin's lymphoma reoccur after so many years?

Our initial reaction after the shock was, "This will be okay, you will have the chemotherapy and life will go on." Life did go on but not as we had imagined. This disease would turn our lives upside-down. It would lead to him having to relinquish his position as a senior pastor of a small congregation, and he would no longer be able to work at his secular job as a senior systems engineer.

Our livelihood was threatened and our plans for the future were at risk. We had two daughters to put through college. I had left full-time nursing after the girls were born, and for the past seventeen years Scott had been the primary provider for our family. We had left Maryland five years prior to relocate to Florida, and I was no longer working, not even part-time.

His illness pulled on our faith for physical healing as well as for daily provision. Unbeknownst to us, we were getting ready to experience a trust and reliance on God that we had never experienced before. All of our years in ministry, our walk with God, what we had heard and taught would be tested. Faith in God is not something that we only speak out of our mouths, but every Christian's faith will be tested. James 1:3 reads that the testing of our faith produces perseverance. If we are to stand in difficult times, our faith must be tested to produce in us what we will need to stand.

Prior to the accident and the MRI, Scott had experienced no cancer-related symptoms of any kind. I recall a friend asking me before we were married if I was concerned that his cancer might come back. Call me naïve but it never entered my mind that he would be diagnosed with cancer a second time. After all, when we met he had been cancer-free for nearly fifteen years. In my mind the chances of him having cancer were no greater than my chances or the chances of anyone else.

Because thirty-one years had passed since his first diagnosis, the physicians deemed this a new cancer. Preparation to receive chemotherapy was started right away. After three cycles of chemotherapy the cancer appeared to get worse. It was not responding to the therapy;

the cancer had spread further. His treatment was changed to another chemotherapy, which required him to be inpatient. He would receive around the clock chemotherapy for five to six days every three weeks. After two cycles of the new chemotherapy regimen, re-staging scans were done and showed improvement. He would need to complete two more cycles and then we would look at starting the process for an autologous stem cell transplant. Autologous means that the transplant is done with the patient using his own stem cells. The goal is for the chemotherapy to put the patient in remission. While the patient is in remission, his cells are harvested and prepared for transplant at a later date.

The first step in preparation for the bone marrow transplant is vital organ testing. All of the major organs in the body are tested to ensure the patient's overall health is good. The organs need to be at optimal health to withstand the exhausting process of recovering from a stem cell transplant. The testing of the vital organs are long days with many appointments and the timing must be carefully coordinated with the ultimate goal of a stem cell transplant in mind.

We started our journey through the vital organ testing protocol. This process began with a chest x-ray. Then, an electrocardiogram was done to record his heart rate and establish a baseline. A multiple gated acquisition scan was performed to further assess if the chemotherapy drugs had damaged the heart or valves in any way. This scan would show how well the heart was pumping blood. A pulmonary function test measured how well the lungs were functioning. Blood work to evaluate the kidneys and other organs were completed.

We had to visit with the social worker and a caseworker to make sure we had the support systems we needed in-place. He also met with a psychologist; all of this is done to determine the physical, emotional, financial, and mental ability of the patient. The stem cell transplant is a long, risky, and debilitating process. It takes a strong person, physically and mentally to withstand the grueling process of recovery.

Other visits prior to the transplant are with the physician assistant in the bone marrow transplant unit. A carefully scheduled bone marrow biopsy was done before the harvesting of his stem cells began. If the marrow showed malignant cells, then he couldn't use his own stem cells. The bone marrow needs to be clear of cancer cells before the harvesting can begin.

The patient and the caregiver are required to meet with the transplant nurse and transplant physician, who discusses the results of the vital organ testing and explains the details of the transplant. At this appointment, we received the report that his heart, lungs, and kidneys were all in excellent condition and the latest bone marrow biopsy was clean. Scott was an outstanding candidate for the stem cell transplant.

All parties appeared to be ready and the bone marrow transplant was scheduled. We had come so far and were feeling hopeful that this would soon be in our distant memory. But we encountered one unexpected challenge. A challenge we never thought about; we did not see this one coming.

On Christmas Eve 2008, we received a denial from the insurance company regarding the stem cell transplant. We learned that our insurance company used certain designated transplant centers and would not pay for the procedure to be done at a non-designated transplant center. These designated centers were all great transplant centers, but unfortunately for us none of them were located in the state of Florida. In order to have the transplant, the patient and the caregiver would have to travel to a center outside of the state and be prepared to stay in that area where the transplant was performed for six to eight weeks. This timeline is based on the assumption that the transplant goes well and that there are no complications.

This news was very disappointing to us, and at that moment going out of state for the transplant did not seem possible. It was during the school year and our two daughters at the time were in school: one in middle school and the other in high school. Their lives had been disrupted enough by their father's illness and we did not wish to misplace them anymore than necessary. Also, the extra out-of-pocket cost for having to live somewhere else for six to eight weeks was not something we were financially in a position to do without tapping into our savings.

We were already in a situation where the out-of-pocket medical expenses exceeded what we could afford, and we did not wish to liquidate any assets, at least not this early in the process. The issues aligned with having to travel for the transplant were more than we could mentally process at the time with everything else that was going on.

We began the appeals process with the insurance company, and our prayer was that the insurance company would agree to cover the procedure at Moffitt Cancer Center. Moffitt is one of the top cancer centers in the United States, and we lived less than twenty-five minutes away. It did not make sense for us to have to travel for a procedure that could be done right near our home where he had been receiving treatment all along.

When we moved to Florida a few years prior, the home we purchased was located near Moffitt Cancer Research Center. Little did we know at the time that we would become frequent visitors to that facility. Because we serve a sovereign God, I believe He placed us right where we needed to be for this upset in our lives. And we believed that He would work it out so that the transplant could be done at that facility.

While we were waiting to hear a decision regarding our appeals, Scott continued the inpatient chemotherapy. The around the clock, five to six days of chemotherapy was hard on his body. There were problems with each treatment and abnormal labs that required additional treatment. He encountered several expected complications and some unexpected ones requiring blood transfusions, potassium infusions, and additional medication.

This was an extremely stressful time for us, not only was my husband sick, but now we had to deal with when, if, and how he could get the treatment he needed. There was nothing we could do but wait. We had no choice but to trust that God was in control. Knowing that God had not abandoned His plan for our lives brought us great comfort.

Stem Cell Transplant

The delay in receiving a decision from the insurance company presented its own set of difficulties. The trouble with the delay was that while the patient is in remission, the stem cells need to be harvested. Restaging and vital organ testing would need to be done again if we waited too long. An added challenge we faced in the meantime was that too much chemotherapy could damage the bone marrow and the patient would not be a candidate for the transplant. And if we waited and did not continue chemotherapy, the patient can come out of remission. Timing was very important as we waited to hear back from the insurance company while carefully monitoring the risk of receiving or not receiving chemotherapy.

On January 5, 2009, we were approved to have the stem cell transplant done at Moffitt Cancer Center in Tampa, Florida. A positron emission tomography (PET scan) and computerized axial tomography (CAT scan) were scheduled to make sure everything was still stable. These tests would look at the internal organs as compared with previous exams. These results would let us know if more chemotherapy was needed or if we could proceed in rescheduling the transplant. The other component was that the bone marrow needed time to recover from the chemotherapy he had received before they could begin harvesting his stem cell for transplant.

Thankfully, the CAT scan and the PET scan were stable, no change. No more chemotherapy was needed, and a second port was inserted to be used for harvesting and transplanting the stem cells. The pre-stem cell transplant meetings continued as scheduled with the transition nurse to learn everything we needed to know about cell harvesting and transplanting, along with one last visit with the transplant physician to sign the consent forms.

I was required to attend classes regarding food preparation and caring for a post-transplant patient. My training as a registered nurse would provide me a level of comfort while caring for a transplant patient, but it did not excuse me from the necessary classes all caregivers were required to take. Certainly, my skills would come in handy but I could not substitute them for what I needed to learn to take care of my husband post-transplant.

We would have to keep our home environment as germ-free as humanly possible. I also had to sign paperwork committing to the fact that I would be responsible for his care upon discharge. I had to designate an alternate caregiver just in case I became ill during his recovery. I would not be permitted to care for him if I developed a cold, sore throat, or fever. Thankfully, my husband's aunt agreed to come from Maryland to assist us during this time. She would be a welcome addition to the household for certain. Even in the most difficult times God always provides help. We had many friends and family who rallied around us to support and pray for us. I am convinced it was because of the prayers of so many people that God moved on our behalf opening the door for him to have his transplant done locally with no other delays.

The stem cell collection process can take a few days. On the first day, he was connected to the machine for five hours. Blood work post collection showed some depletion of potassium and magnesium, which had to be replenished. On day two of collection, they were able to collect enough stem cells for the transplant. Potassium and magnesium had to be replenished again on day two.

The harvesting procedure was tough for him. The insertion of the special intravenous catheter and all that goes into preparing a patient for harvesting can be uncomfortable. As I sat at his bedside observing, I gained a new appreciation for those who donate stem cells and their experience. If my husband endured this struggle to donate his own cells to save his own life, I only have one word for those who donate for others. That word is amazing. People who set their own agendas aside and donate to improve the quality of life of others are remarkable human beings. Many who donate have no idea who will receive their life-saving gift, but they donate regardless. I am thankful to God for people who care enough to give the gift of life. It is truly a blessing to have people on this earth who will put the needs of others before their own. May God bless them for being unselfish and for caring enough to do something for another human being. There are many gracious, giving individuals who donate to people they will never meet. Donors give without recognition or appreciation, looking for nothing in return.

A few days before the transplant, we had one last clearance appointment. The physician went over any last-minute details and answered the questions we had. The harvesting collected 2.93 million cells. At least 2 million stem cells are needed for a transplant. We were informed that one year after the stem cell transplant, the patient will need to receive all of his childhood immunizations again. Antivirals will need to be taken for the first year until the immunizations have begun.

The pre-transplant therapy will destroy the immune system, and then the new stem cells will be implanted. Once the new stem cells are implanted, the immune system will start to recover. It was a blessing that Scott could donate his own cells. Receiving your own cells lowers the concern of rejection. I do not like to say never but we did not anticipate that his body would reject its own cells. We had met some patients along the way who received stem cells from donors and were very familiar with the problems that could develop should rejection become a problem. Thankfully, this was one less thing we had to be concerned about.

The next step was waiting for a bed at the hospital. A few days later we received a call from the admitting office that a bed was available. On February 11, 2009, Scott was admitted to the hospital to begin the process. The day of admission is called minus day five. The days are counted in minuses with the transplant day being day zero. Conditioning chemotherapy is given on the minus days with a rest day before the transplant. On day zero, the stem cells are transplanted.

The newly constructed bone marrow transplant wing at Moffitt Cancer Center was set to open in a few days. To our surprise Scott was moved to the brand new bone marrow transplant unit for his transplant, he was the first transplant patient in the new unit.

The stem cell transplant is done at the bedside. The prepared stem cells are infused into the body using the same catheter that was inserted at the base of his neck into his right jugular vein for the harvesting of the stem cells. A physician along with the nurse is present during the procedure. During the transplant, his blood pressure spiked requiring medication. We were told in advance that this could happen so the team was prepared.

The preservatives used to keep the stem cells until transplant have a distinct odor. The patient cannot smell it, but everyone who enters the room can smell the chemicals, an aroma reminding me of an opened can of corn.

Stem Cell Transplant

The first night was uneventful, but by morning the labs had started to drop. The white counts along with other blood values would need to drop, and then the immune system will slowly start to rebuild.

On day two his labs continued to drop, and he experienced fatigue and loss of appetite. It is very important during this time that the patient does not become dehydrated. On day three, he continued to receive intravenous fluid to combat dehydration. His white count and platelet count also continued to drop. In addition to the extreme fatigue, he complained of abdominal pain.

We were previously told that day three, four, and five would be the most challenging. With this in mind, we knew the worst was yet to come. During this time, he mostly stayed in bed except for the required physical therapy. Despite the fatigue, it is necessary that the patient be as mobile as possible.

One of the things the transplant physician told me was that when he gets home, I would have to make sure he got out of bed. With the fatigue, there is the propensity to lie down. My chore was to see that he did not spend too much time in bed. My husband was always an early riser, and for years I wanted him to just lie in bed on Saturday morning so we could get some extra sleep. Now I was being told that the one who likes to lie in bed had to be the one to encourage the early riser to get up. It would take effort on my part, but I was committed to being the best caregiver possible.

During his hospitalization for the transplant, there had been some talk about early discharge for him. The initial discharge date was delayed because both girls were sick and he would not be allowed to come home. We understood that once discharge had taken place, he would need to come back to the clinic each day for lab work and correction of any abnormal lab results. The daily outpatient visits could be anywhere from four to eight hours, depending on what he needed on any given day.

He could possibly need infusions, transfusions, or other medication. This information helps to explain why the out-of-state transplant centers required the patient and caregiver to stay in the area 6 to 8 weeks post-transplant. Thankfully, the insurance issue was resolved, and we did not have to travel for the procedure.

This entire process has given me a stronger appreciation for the Word of God. In Scripture, we read of God's great love and how He knows all the challenges we face in life. He had already gone before us to prepare everything we needed. Our stress and worrying are wasted emotions for we must trust God. God had indeed gone before us to put everything in place that we would need for the journey. Even when we did not understand, He was working things out for our good according to His plan and purpose for us.

Post-discharge instructions would also include exercising extreme precaution. Good hand washing techniques for all needed to be practiced, and he would have to wear a mask when around other people. The food preparation classes I took prepared me for making his meals at home. No leftovers and food would need to be eaten soon after preparation. Anything raw had to be scrubbed and triple-washed. We were also instructed not to have any pets, fresh flowers, or plants in the house.

Often when patients are sent home soon after the transplant, it is with the knowledge that they will need to return to the hospital if they develop a fever. A fever may occur around day four when engraftment starts to take place. Engraftment is when the new blood-forming cells begin to grow and make healthy blood cells.

Because of our girls being sick with colds, we missed the window for discharge for him, and by day four, his appetite was extremely poor and he was showing signs of dehydration. The intravenous fluids were increased. It was surreal to see that blood count numbers could go so low and a person still be alive. The nurses write the numbers on the board in the patient's room to encourage the patient as the cells start to recover.

On day seven, the platelet counts did recover some, but they were still too low for discharge. He was given platelets and the intravenous fluid continued. Because his appetite remained poor, intravenous hydration was of the uppermost importance. As a result of not eating, his blood pressure dropped and his weight was down. The goal was elevation in his white count and improvement in his diet so he could be discharged. It is proven that patients recover better at home and the risk of infection decreases outside of the hospital. Being a former nurse I knew all too well the assortment of germs that lurk in hospitals. The bone marrow unit is most likely the least germy unit in a hospital, but it is still a hospital.

Scott was discharged on the evening of day nine. The staff made a big banner that read congratulations. The patient runs through the banner and breaks it on their way out of the bone marrow transplant ward.

Our home was ready to receive him. The girls had been instructed that once they entered the house after school, they needed to change clothes and wash their hands.

The morning of day ten, we had our first post discharge clinic visit. On our daily trips to the clinic, he did require transfusions, infusions, and medication. The first visit was about a six-hour day. I was so thankful that his aunt was here. It meant so much to have another adult in the house. Having someone to help with the girls and just to have company meant so much to me. I cannot express how important it is for a caregiver to have that kind of support.

With each clinic visit, his condition continued to improve. His blood work became more normal requiring less replenishing of blood and other body chemistries. On day seventeen, we had a follow-up visit with the transplant physician and were told that engraftment had taken place. Engraftment meant that the transplanted stem cells have started to grow and make new blood cells. This whole process is rather remarkable and to see it up close is extra amazing.

An appointment was scheduled to remove the special catheter that was put in for harvesting and transplanting the stem cells. Scott described it as being extremely painful. During the procedure, his blood pressure spiked and attempts to remove the catheter were momentarily aborted, but it was eventually successfully removed.

Our daily clinic visits went to weekly visits. Anytime we were out in public Scott had to wear a mask. He was instructed to stay out of crowds avoiding small children and sick people. His immune system was compromised, and it was trying to rebuild itself.

On day thirty, restaging with a PET and CAT scan was done to let us know if the transplant had cleared his body of the cancer. Unfortunately, we did not get the news we were hoping for; I fully expected the doctor to tell us that Scott was cancer-free. But instead there were suspicious findings on the scans. We had come so far but our journey was not over yet. Even in the disappointing news our faith remained strong. We stood on all that we knew to be true about God. He is not a man that He should lie (Numbers 23:19) and that He promised never to leave us (Deuteronomy 31:6). We knew Him to be a healer of all disease (Psalm 103:3), and we had to continue to look to Him as the great physician. Scott had been through so much already, but we remained hopeful that things would work out well for him.

On day sixty-six post-transplant my mother died. She had been diagnosed shortly before my husband with non-Hodgkin lymphoma, another form of cancer that originates in the lymphatic system. As a result of my responsibilities as his caregiver, I was unable to visit my mother as often as I would have liked. Thankfully, my siblings were there to assist her during the final days of her life here on earth.

Stem Cell Transplant

My mother's death on April 22, 2009, took me on a solo trip to North Carolina. The last time I had visited her was several months prior when my husband's aunt and uncle came to Florida for a visit. While they were visiting with him, I took a trip to visit with my mother. My mother and I spoke on the phone often, and she offered encouragement to me as I cared for my husband.

The drive to North Carolina to prepare for her funeral permitted me time for reflection on things past and present. I was comforted knowing my mother was now at peace and free from pain and disease.

Prior to me leaving for North Carolina to arrange my mother's funeral, Scott had a doctor's appointment. During the appointment, a chest x-ray was done because he had a cough. When I returned to Florida after the funeral, his cough was worse. I immediately contacted the physician and was told that the chest x-ray revealed ground glass pneumonia. Dealing with the death of my mother, my husband's illness, and why no one called us regarding the abnormal chest x-ray proved frustrating. But there was no time for lingering in frustration as the pneumonia had to be treated.

The doctor ordered antibiotics and antifungal drugs. A few days later, a bronchoscopy using a thin viewing instrument to look at his airway was done to take a closer look but the bronchi washing did not show any fungus. While dealing with the pneumonia surprise, one of our daughters got the flu. She was one of many students who were infected with the flu virus, and her school was closed for a week for outbreak of possible swine flu cases. Now I was dealing with the grief of losing my mother, taking care of my husband with pneumonia, and taking care of a sick child while trying to sanitize our home of the flu virus.

Amid multiple challenges, life has to continue. Our lives became a daily test figuring out how we would make it from one day to the next. Stress levels were high and staying focused was difficult. But all of this would be worth it to hear that he was cancer-free.

Cancer or No Cancer

On day ninety-nine, the post-transplant visit to the physician revealed that Scott was in remission. Whatever was seen on the PET and CAT scan two months ago had resolved itself. The plan was to check again in three months. If the tests were normal, then he would be rechecked every six months for the next four years. After the five-year mark, the restaging exams would be once a year.

Scott did recover from the cancer and returned to work twenty-two months after the stem cell transplant. Just as we were settling into what appeared to be our old life, something drastic happened.

Ten months after returning to work, he lost the use of his legs rendering him unable to stand or walk. An MRI revealed lesions inside of his spinal cord. After much discussion of what it might be, it was decided that a biopsy of the spinal cord was in order. The physicians' opinions vacillated between scar tissue, radiation induced spinal cord necrosis, lymphoma, or another kind of spinal tumor. The surgeon explained the risk involved in spinal cord surgery, but my husband wanted answers.

After the procedure, the surgeon still was not sure of what it was, but he stated that he did not believe it was cancer. The pathology report confirmed this and the lesions in the spinal cord disappeared with intravenous steroids. It was determined that he had developed an autoimmune disease affecting the spinal cord.

After the hospital discharge, Scott was sent to an inpatient rehabilitation center where he spent three weeks. Upon his return home, he required in-home physical therapy. Eventually graduating to outpatient therapy, he continued to progress.

To see him admitted to a rehabilitation facility was an unimaginable moment for me. Filled with thoughts of what will I do once he comes home? What if he never walks again? His progress was remarkable; to see him start out wheelchair bound and learn to walk was truly a God moment. By the time he was discharged, he could walk short distances with the four-leg walker. After much therapy and prayer, he was walking again with the assistance of only a cane.

Although he was walking, he suffered debilitating pain. His skin was hypersensitive to touch. At times, it was painful for his clothes to touch his skin. What a miserable way to live each day. This would begin our quest for answers but everywhere we looked led to more questions.

We eventually saw a neurologist at the Mayo Clinic in Jacksonville, Florida, who diagnosed him with neuromyelitis optica-like (NMO) symptoms. Neuromyelitis optica is also known as Devic's disease. This disease affects the central nervous system, primarily the eye nerves and the spinal cord. Like other autoimmune diseases, the body's immune system fights against its own cells. The cause of NMO is not known and has often been misdiagnosed as multiple sclerosis. There is no cure for the disease but the symptoms of pain and other muscle problems can be managed.

One year later, he experienced paralysis again. This time the paralysis and numbing sensations had moved upward from his legs to his abdomen and chest area. An MRI revealed a lesion in his cervical spine. He was once again treated with intravenous steroids and other medications. He was discharged to an inpatient rehabilitation center, from there he came home to receive home physical therapy and finally to outpatient therapy.

While he did not experience permanent vision loss, it was clear that he did have a majority of the symptoms of NMO, a debilitating disease. He had to wear gloves because any object he touched felt very cold. He went through a period when no one could touch him; even the bed linens touching his body were painful. Nerve pain is difficult to treat.

On another hospital admission, it was revealed that he had pleural effusion, fluid in his chest. Because of the weakness of his chest wall muscles he was unable to take deep breaths. And because of this, excessive fluid builds up in his lungs. He would now be required to sleep with a machine at night that would force air into his lungs. A hospital bed was also required so he could raise his head to a level of comfort. In addition to this news, we were told that because his chest wall muscles were so weak, he no longer could travel by air.

With the lesion appearing in his cervical spinal cord, anything below that area can be affected including his respiratory system. This was a particularly tense time for us with not knowing if he would recover. Once again, we witnessed a powerful move of God through prayer. Scott is a resilient individual who continues to move forward despite all he had been through.

We have experienced many hurdles along the way. Because of his never-ending pain, there was discussion among the medical staff of sending him to a hospice house for pain control. After prayer and conversation, we decided that he would recover better at home. As his caregiver, I go back and forth wondering if I have made the right decision but ultimately I had to learn to release it to God. Our lives are in His hand and He is the one who determines the number of our days. At that point in Scott's life, the benefits of him coming home outweighed the benefits of him going into hospice. I believe we will know when he is ready for hospice and this was not the time.

EMOTIONAL ROLLERCOASTER

See Me Hear Me Know Me

Caregiver's Grieving Heart

"Cast all your anxiety on him because he cares for you"
(1 Peter 5:7).

Caregiver's grief is similar to the grief survivors experience when they lose a loved one. Many caregivers begin the grieving process before their loved one passes away. With the initial diagnosis comes the shock and disbelief. The spouse caregiver will grieve for the person they once knew. Spouses will grieve the loss of the relationship as it once was. An extended illness can change a person and not always for good. Not only does the ill person experience change, but others around them can become casualties of the change. Some of the changes experienced may include physical body changes. However, the emotional and mental personality may be altered as well. A once vibrant, exciting person with the brokenness of body and spirit can become sad and withdrawn which can lead to a state of depression.

Once an individual has been diagnosed with a long-term illness, that person must cope with the fact that they can no longer perform their daily tasks. This change alone can be depressing for many patients and for their caregiving spouses.

For many who are suffering, simple things like walking and talking can no longer be taken for granted. The caregiver must deal with the reality that they have lost the person they once knew. The healthy family member is now the ill family member, and it seems as if everything revolves around the illness. The illness takes on a life of its own and can consume the entire family. Everything is planned around the ill person and their needs. With all the changes, it is easy for caregivers to get lost in their duties and neglect their own needs.

The grieving process for those who are left behind traditionally begins at the end of a loved one's life. But when the illness goes on year after year, the stages of grief may be halted and linger for many years. I have watched my husband go from the energetic man I married to someone who periodically stays in the bed for days and may only leave the house for doctor's appointments. I grieved for myself, for him, and for our children knowing that his life has changed forever. As a result of his life changing, so has ours.

When caring for a loved one, coming to terms with your new normal will be necessary. You will be able to read more about this later in the book. Just as when someone dies and we eventually accept what has happened, a caregiver must do the same. Coming to terms with what has been lost is difficult when your loved one is still alive. When you observe the suffering of your loved one up-close and personal, it can lead to much sorrow. It becomes somewhat traumatic for the caregiving spouses as they prepare for death repeatedly. With each hospital admission, our initial reaction was to wonder if this would be "it."

On one of my husband's hospitalizations, the nurse helped him to the chair and left the room. The call bell was not where he could reach it, and he tried to get back to bed without assistance. He fell to the floor. That was the first of many times he would fall, and I questioned if this would be his end. The frequent falls would inevitably lead to a fracture or some form of head trauma, I thought. The anticipation of bad news while hoping for good news becomes the normal thought pattern for spouses who are caregivers. Continually preparing and wondering what is coming next each time the physician enters the room.

The caregivers must come to terms with the unstableness of their new life. It does not benefit anyone to wish things would return to normal. We can and should continue to pray trusting that God has a better plan, but wishing does not change anything. The grieving family of a terminally ill patient will need to be able to process what they are feeling in a way that is productive for their lives. People may not understand, but as each family experiences their own victories and defeats, they will need to deal with their experiences in a way that promotes wholeness of body, soul, and mind.

A person who is caring for an ill spouse will need to find things to do that they both enjoy. Going out to the movies may prove difficult, but you can watch movies at home. Find ways to create new experiences by finding things you can do together. Try to develop better communication skills as you will be spending a lot of time together. It is essential that you as the caregiver as well as the ill spouse remain as sociable as possible during this process. Being able to socialize with friends and family will help you both to process the grief. Being able to share with others what you are feeling will be particularly beneficial.

Many caregivers experience guilt, wondering what they could have done differently. I struggled with guilt. I would feel guilty when my husband would have any kind of flare up in his condition. I would wonder if I had missed something that I should have caught sooner. I pondered if I should have insisted that he eat even when he said he did not want to. My clinical background of nursing added to my harsh judgement of myself.

One year, I had a cold and when my husband began to show symptoms; the guilt set in. Because of his weakened immune system, he is especially vulnerable to infections. We always tried to be particularly careful with him around sick people, but sometimes it just cannot be avoided. As a result of the respiratory symptoms he developed, he was taken to the hospital. A CAT scan of the chest revealed a large amount of fluid in his chest and fluid around his heart. As strange as it may sound that diagnosis offered me some relief of the guilt feelings I was experiencing. Pleural effusion was something that he had problems with in the past, and I thought that it was not cold-related but related to his underlying autoimmune disease. But because of his weak immune system, any insult was the potential for a greater problem. Being a caregiver who struggled with guilt, this only magnified what I was already feeling. What could I have done differently to protect him from being exposed?

After more than twenty-five days in the hospital with pleural and cardiac effusion, his cardiologist decided the fluid around the heart had been there for several years and was stable. He did not wish to offer any intervention related to that at the time. The lung fluid did require immediate intervention which included a surgical procedure. Additional complications, some related to the surgery and some not, landed him in the intensive care unit for several days.

What I learned from this challenge was that guilt serves no productive purpose. God is in control and only He knows the whys of our well-being. I was determined to become free of feeling guilty but I knew I could not do it alone.

There were times when I felt guilty about being healthy and even wished I was the one who was ill. I felt I somehow could deal with illness better than he could. When my husband would complain, I attempted to make him feel better by saying, "It's going to be all right." And he would respond, "You don't understand how I feel." His comments only served to increase my feelings of guilt. There were times when I wondered if he resented me for being healthy.

I would feel guilty about not staying with him during his hospitalizations. He wanted me to be there when the doctors came by, but the doctors' rounding schedule was unpredictable. I would feel guilty about going home at night to rest or doing things with my friends. Even though he would say go ahead, his mannerism did not support what was coming from his mouth. He would follow the "Go ahead and go" with "I wish I could go places like you." I believe what he was really saying was that he had a desire to do things that he could no longer do. But in my guilt-ridden state, his words only served as a reminder to me that I had freedoms that he no longer enjoyed.

Guilt is a wasted emotion. Nevertheless, it was my constant companion. Finally, I came to terms with the fact that there were many things in life that I could not control. I could not go through life avoiding things simply because I did not want to feel bad later. I would do the best I could to make sure my husband was as safe and healthy as possible. But I had to understand that God was in control of our lives, and He makes the final decisions concerning what happens and what does not. I understood that if I denied myself out of guilt, it would only serve to produce resentment in me later. If I neglected to do some of the things that brought me joy, I would later blame my husband for decisions that I made. He would be the reason I gave up every part of my life, and I did not want feelings of resentment in my future. I knew that if I ended up resenting my husband that would only serve to produce feelings of guilt later because of the feelings of resentment I felt during his illness. It is a vicious cycle that can take full control over one's life if allowed. That was not what I wanted for my life, and I am sure as caregivers, the same would be true for your life.

Through much prayer and introspection, I began to realize that the guilt I experienced was caused by the fact that I held myself to an impossibly high standard. I did not want to permit myself to make mistakes. I felt that I had to do everything perfectly and would accept nothing less of myself. I wanted to be the picture-perfect wife caregiver. I was setting myself up for failure and misery and that was not something I wanted to do. I had to release it to God.

As a wife caregiver, I had to accept the fact that God was in control of both my life and my husband's. I had to come to the conclusion that there were many things neither one of us could control. Every human being makes mistakes, and there was no way I would be perfect in my pursuit. I could not go through life second-guessing every decision I made, but I had to rest in God knowing that He had already gone before me and knew everything that I would encounter in this life.

Caregivers can only do their best. We must learn not to stress about things that we cannot control. Making mistakes is what makes us human and just as we forgive others, we must be willing to forgive ourselves. I did not have control over my catching a cold, and I certainly did not have control over him picking up the virus. We lived in the same house and I could do my best with hand washing and other precautions, but ultimately God was in control. I had to admit that my feelings of guilt were not valid and that I must allow myself to be free of them.

Guilt can be a trick that satan uses to cause those who love God to wallow in fear and doubt. If I stressed about what I was feeling in regards to my husband, I would be limited in my ability to care for him. Guilt can be a consuming emotion rendering the caregiver emotionally delicate. Jesus' death and resurrection freed us from guilt and shame, and we as believers can walk with our heads up knowing that He is the regulator of it all even as we care for our loved ones.

Moving past the feelings of guilt and getting to a place of peace is necessary for the caregiver. Although my husband would no longer do things he had done in the past, I had to nurture myself by doing some of the things I enjoyed. I accepted our situation as it currently was. I could not create a fantasy of being a caregiver. Our lives were interrupted by his illness and that was something we had to confront daily. It was not the future we planned, but it was and is our reality. After all, if I was the one who was ill, I certainly would not want him to give up everything he enjoyed to sit and guard me every day, all day. I am thankful that I am physically able to care for him, and yes, it can be rewarding but also challenging to be his caregiver.

Realizing that I alone could not manage what was happening to my husband was a defining moment for me. I understood that the only thing I could control was how I reacted to what happened to him. I must admit I was a few years into the caregiver's journey before I reconciled all of this in my mind. I still slip up from time to time, but my message to all is to know that life is meant to be lived to the best of our abilities. I did not have to stop living because my husband became ill. I had to curtail many things and even sacrifice some things, but I did not have to remove myself from society. What purpose would that serve? Life is meant for the living and even though I am a caregiver, I am still among the living and frankly, so is he.

The caregiver may experience anger, questioning, "Why did this happen?" Be careful with the "Why me?" This can lead to depression because there are no real answers. As I write this book, I think I am in the acceptance stage of caregiver's grief. This does not mean that I am pleased with the state of our lives, but it means that I have accepted my husband's condition as a chapter in our lives. It is a long chapter, but I must remember it is only a part of our story. I accepted the fact that the flow of our lives has changed. My husband is ill, and I cannot expect him to behave as a healthy man. His travel abilities are limited, and physical activity is exhausting for him.

If I had the choice, I would definitely select to never have traveled this road, but the choice was neither mine nor his. I no longer think about his death and what that would mean, but I think more about living the best life I can live, because death could come to me before it comes to him. I have known too many women to die shortly after the husband they cared for passed away. Caregivers know better than most about how uncertain life can be. Experiencing my husband's illness has prompted me to look at life differently.

I feel that I am better prepared for life's challenges because of what I have experienced with my husband. Our children are better prepared as they have a close and personal view of sickness. They have a stronger resolve to live their best life because they understand how uncertain life can be. They witnessed their father becoming ill at an early age. Our family dialogs more freely about death and dying and what that means to those we leave behind. We have learned to say to each other what needs to be said, not putting off today for tomorrow so that we each can live life free of regrets.

Confess any guilt you may be experiencing and pray asking God to deliver you.

Use your accompanying journal to write what you are feeling after you have prayed.

Heart of Contentment

"But if we have food and clothing, we will be content with that"
(1 Timothy 6:8).

Contentment is a skill that, if learned, can relieve stress and anxiety. Being satisfied mentally or emotionally is something we strive to obtain. You may wonder as I have many times, "How can anyone be content as a caregiver?" How can a person obtain satisfaction from caring for a loved one who is ill? There is a hint of satisfaction in caring for a loved one, but there are many components of the caregiver's life that are absent as a result of caring for a loved one with a chronic illness. Funds are depleted, medical expenses are high, something is always lacking, and life as you once knew it has changed. Sleepless nights and stressful days become the norm. With all the changes to one's life because of illness, how can the caregiver discover contentment?

As a caregiver, when you look at the dreams you had for your life and the life of your loved one, discontentment can occur. Now because of your new role, none of the things you once dreamed seem possible. What you are experiencing at this time in your life is not what you imagined life would be like. Things have changed. Many caregivers have left careers to care for their loved one. Abandoning a career will mean a decrease in the finances. In many cases, it can also lead to a damaged self-esteem, because we as humans often equate who we are with what we do. Our self-worth can be diminished when we no longer receive monetary compensation.

With the decrease in finances, the organization of the family is altered. Things that were once enjoyed may have to be limited or omitted. In some cases, children have to abandon their dreams to go to college because they need to enter the workforce. They must find work because there is no money for college as a result of major medical expenses and reduced income. Cars and home loans have been defaulted upon. The surmounting medical expenses have forced some families even into bankruptcy.

For many families, the person who becomes ill is the primary provider for the family. This can be extremely difficult when the spouse who is now the caregiver and has not worked for many years has to reenter the workforce. Or because of caregivers' responsibilities, the caregiving spouse is unable to return to work. This can be an anxiety producing time. So how does one discover contentment?

How is the word contentment defined? Is contentment simply accepting one's fate in life? Does contentment mean that a person has settled into the new role, accepted the good and the bad while believing this is all there is to life? There is a difference between settling and being content. While one may have settled into life, it does not mean that the individual is happy or content.

Contentment has to do with accepting where you are in life at this moment. It does not mean that you do not aspire toward something better or greater. It does mean that you refuse to blame someone else for where you are, and you reject the notion to give up because of your present circumstances.

Contentment has less to do with our situation and more to do with our state of mind. Contentment is more about being free from worry and anxiety in a current situation. Feeling at peace and satisfied about whatever state you find yourself in at any given moment means that you are content.

The contentment that a caregiver experiences is not from the external circumstances, but it comes from an understanding that we are not in control of our lives or the lives of the ones we care for. A caregiver can experience freedom from anxiety by accepting what is happening today, but believing that tomorrow can be better.

Contentment is not being happy about the condition of your life, but it is about trusting the One who holds your life and the life of the one you care for. Contentment comes from knowing that God has predestined your life and He is concerned with everything that concerns you, so He will not leave you stranded. Because you know that your God is all-knowing, you must accept that He knew your future before you showed up on the earth.

As a caregiver, you must embrace your new normal. There are so many things that will be out of your control, but your role as a caregiver will create new routines in your life. Both patient and caregiver will face an array of emotions. Caregivers do not only have responsibility for themselves but also for the person they care for.

The struggle to retain some control of life can be stressful. You will need to release what you cannot change to God. The burden of everything will be too much for you to carry. God is in control of everything including you and the loved one you care for.

It is important to maintain balance and evaluate the changes. It will be necessary to accept what has happened because chronic illness is not something that we can control. The fight to change something that we cannot change will only serve to frustrate us.

In our effort to secure contentment, the caregiver must realize that some things may not get done and that the sun will still shine tomorrow. The housework may have to wait so that caregivers can take care of themselves as well as the loved ones they care for. Learning to be content with not doing the laundry or washing the dishes is a goal that is obtainable. You can try again tomorrow. Learn to be kind to yourself. Decline to set unrealistic expectations. You will not be able to do everything; do not try to be a super caregiver. If someone offers to help, learn to accept the help and be satisfied with the job they do. Others may not do things exactly how you like them done, but their efforts should be applauded and accepted.

As a caregiver, during the day, many things will happen that may ignite frustration. The challenge is to surrender it to the Holy Spirit and not try to handle it on our own. I can testify that every time I try to manage trials on my own the outcome is less than desirable. Learning to release things to God knowing that we cannot control everything can be challenging at those times but that is what we need to do, nonetheless.

When my husband goes in the hospital, we lose all sense of control. Doctors always stress to patients the importance of taking their medication correctly. It is always interesting to me how medication regiments get mixed up when a person is admitted to the hospital.

On my husband's most recent admission, I went over his at home medications with the emergency room nurse and physician. When we got to the unit, we went over them again with the admitting nurse. The next day we discovered the medications were being given incorrectly. We went over them again with the night nurse and the doctor who works in the hospital caring for patients on the units. When Scott moved to progressive care, we went over them again. When they transferred him to intensive care, we reviewed the medications again with that nurse. On the third day, he was transferred to another hospital to cardiac care unit. There we went over his medication again with the staff at the new hospital only to discover that some of his medications that we brought in from home were not transferred to the second hospital with him.

Adding to my already hectic schedule, the hospital requested that I come back to retrieve the left behind medication. It was a controlled substance and could only be released to me with my signature. Exhausted, I pleaded with the hospital to allow me to send a family member to retrieve the medication. Fortunately, the nursing supervisor agreed, and I sent my brother to retrieve the medication.

After spending three days in the cardiac care unit, my husband was transferred to the progressive care unit which required another medication review. I tried to be present for all of the transfers for the purpose of reviewing medication and to ensure nothing was left behind. But with the hospital schedule being so different from the home schedule, quite often things can be confused or omitted. In the middle of all the chaotic rearranging of the patient's schedule, the caregiver and the patient may take on an attitude of grumbling.

Maintaining organization during a hospital stay can be nearly impossible. The caregiver will need to relinquish control and find a place of contentment. Rely on your support team to assist you during this time. Case managers, social workers, chaplains, nursing staff, physicians, etc. are all a part of your healthcare support team. Build a rapport with them as you cannot always be there. I usually write my telephone number on the board in his room and reiterate that I am just a phone call away. I try to be present as shifts change to meet the evening nurse before I go home for the night. It is important to me that she or he knows what I look like and that I know what they look like. People will sometimes feel more connected to you if they have seen your face.

Being my husband's caregiver would often produce discontentment for me. Before he was ill, he knew how to push the right buttons to agitate me. You would think that with twenty-five-plus years of marriage

I would know how not to respond. I guess I am a slow learner. Many times, when I think I am in a place of contentment, his actions can fluster my peaceful place of calm and contentment. It seems to me that his actions are deliberate, but he sees them as unintentional. Either way, I was moved from my place of contentment and would often have to find my way back.

The marriage union has challenges within itself. When you add the role of caregivers, the relationship needs to be redefined. Anyone who has not had the experience of caring for a spouse may not be able to understand the redefining of your roles. Your relationship is unique to what you are experiencing so do not be afraid to make the necessary adjustments.

There are many things that a couple must deal with when one party has a lingering condition. Keeping your marriage together may require help. Being fearful of asking for help is not wise. Seek marital counseling if necessary. Being a caregiver is demanding, so rely on friends and family to assist you. There are some adult care facilities that you may be able to utilize. My husband would never agree to that so we brought in paid help during the early years of his illness. Now after several years of him being ill, our finances have diminished and we are no longer able to bring in paid help.

Accept help wherever and whenever it is offered. You may be able to get someone to help with meals and transporting to appointments. This will permit the caregiver wife time to handle business matters. I cannot tell you the number of hours I spend on the telephone scheduling appointments, dealing with insurance companies, and other business-related matters. I feel like I could teach seminars on all things related to health insurance. So much paperwork, so many forms, so many questions—it is never ending. All of these chores can cause a caregiver to feel discontent. It took me years before I learned to accept the help of social workers. I felt as if I had to know everything, now I realize that social workers are there to assist in understanding the rules of Medicare and the many other agencies.

The effect of illness on a marriage and dealing with the losses can be tremendous. The emotional pain that a caregiver experiences is often difficult to put into words. Facing the loss of a dream—the future you planned together, the expeditions you desired to enjoy, and the events you had planned to attend. And you now find yourself a caregiver to the one who promised to take care of you.

Caregivers will have an added challenge when their loved one has a memory disability. Your life together is built from the memories the two of you have shared and now your loved one does not remember. Illness can wreak havoc on the family unit. The roles become confused and everyone is just trying to survive.

Chronic illness in the family can change the entire dynamics of the family. There may be a role reversal component when the wife is caregiver to her husband. The wife now must take the lead in things the husband would have been responsible for. Added stressors such as taking care of simply household chores like making sure the water purification system salt tank is filled with salt blocks or collecting and putting out the garbage on the right day. These responsibilities can make one feel overwhelmed that they have to do everything.

As caregiver, I felt the burden to oversee the maintenance of the yard, the pool, as well as other household chores. I now had full responsibility for them all. In place of my husband, I was the one climbing the ladders to change high ceiling light bulbs. I needed to know when something was broken, and in some cases, learn to fix things around the house. My husband's chores were now mine, along with the responsibilities I already had, because he was ill.

When illness touches a family, anxiety is heightened by the desire to control mixed with the lack of control. Illness is unpredictable so the fight to control what cannot be controlled is never-ending. We need God's grace to work in our lives to do what we are unable to do for ourselves. His divine influence is imperative in our everyday life as a caregiver if we are going to survive. To discover contentment, we must relinquish control to God.

The situation is out of our control, but we can practice controlling our emotions and actions. Self-control is a fruit of the Spirit that we desperately need operating in our lives daily. In moments of frustration when we are tempted to speak, self-control is required. That can be one of the most difficult things to do, learning to keep our mouths shut. The frustration of caregiving, especially during those times when our loved one is resistant, stirs up the desire to speak.

In the search for contentment some turn to shopping, substance abuse, or eating. Spending, drinking, medication (prescription or non-prescription), overeating, or other things that we look for to satisfy the flesh will not bring the contentment we desire. While these things may bring temporary relief, contentment cannot be found in them.

Exercising self-control can be helpful in dealing with stress and depression which many caregivers will experience. Practicing self-control will assist us in not overspending, overeating, and other escaping habits that may prove damaging in the long run. Discipline will enable us to control our attitude and reject damaging emotions. Self-discipline will reinforce confidence, inner strength, and determination.

In order to achieve contentment, we need to exercise self-control in every area of our lives. We must watch what comes into our hearts, minds, and bodies. We do this by learning to rest in the Lord. When we sense anger, frustration, stress, discontentment or anxiety, we must turn our attention back to God and His Word. It can be so easy to place blame on someone else when things feel out of control. But knowing what God's Word says about our situation can help us be both responsible and disciplined.

Even in the midst of what seems to be hopeless, we can begin to affirm what we already know to be true about God. We know He is all-powerful, and that means that He has control over all things. When you feel yourself losing control, call on the name of Jesus. He will bring you to a place of contentment. Freedom from stress and anxiety is found in God; find that place in Him and rest there.

There are days I have to practice releasing my situation to God over and over again. It is a moment by moment struggle for many caregivers. Many days my focus is just getting through the day and being ready for tomorrow to do it all over again. The job of a caregiver is continuous. It is like being a mom to young children; you are never really off-duty.

I am not satisfied with my husband's condition, but I strive to be content in the circumstances of today. It is a daily choice that I must make each second of every day. Some days the frustration weighs heavily on me, but I make the decision regardless to be content. I realize that tomorrow is not promised, but I trust God that tomorrow will be better.

I am confident that whatever lies ahead God is with me. He never changes. His Word is sure. Isaiah 26:3 reads, "You will keep in perfect peace those whose minds are steadfast, because they trust in you." Our lives may be in turmoil, but if we keep our mind focused, unwavering on God, He will keep our mind in perfect peace. The Hebrew translation for "perfect peace" is "peace peace." This is a greater kind of peace. In order to receive this kind of peace, we must trust in God. Trust means that we commit ourselves fully to God. We are not anxious about the circumstances of life because we are wholly committed to God.

My husband's most recent hospitalization was the most difficult I have experienced to date. With many critical decisions to be made my contentment scale was tilting toward discontentment. It was his first time in this particular facility, and most of the members of his health care team were new to us. The level of comfort we had felt with his past hospitalizations was missing.

This word content speaks of one having a sense of being satisfied. Contentment is not something that comes easy because we always want to focus on how things should be. Apostle Paul writes in Scripture that he learned to be content (Philippians 4:12). This would mean that Apostle Paul had to experience some disappointments to get him to the place of learning contentment. Like the apostle, we must learn that everything we need is found in our relationship with Christ.

First Timothy 6:6, "But godliness with contentment is great gain." The word contentment in this Scripture relates to having a mind that is satisfied with its portion in life. Coming to the realization that life is brief will aid in the quest for contentment. As a caregiver, I had to make a decision. In this season of my life, I can choose to be disgruntled or content. As 1 Timothy 6:7 notes, "For we brought nothing into the world, and we can take nothing out of it." When caring for a loved one, much of our discontentment is based on how our lives have changed. When we focus on the losses that we have experienced, both physical and emotional discontentment will set in. But remembering that we brought nothing here with us and certainly nothing accompanies us to the graveyard gives clarity to the situation.

Contentment is not found in things. Acknowledging that it is God who provides for us can relieve anxiety about the future. The ability to acquire calm contentment lies beyond our natural abilities. It is not something that we can obtain alone. But we can secure contentment through Christ our Lord.

In our quest to obtain contentment, we must come to a place of accepting that what is happening are lessons for us to learn along the way. Every challenge in our life is meant to bring us to another level of faith in God. Perhaps caring for my husband would teach me some desperately needed life lessons and I must be open in order to learn what they are.

I have been told that illness brings some couples closer together. Some develop a special bond during illness that they would otherwise not have known. When my husband became ill, he had to rely on me for so many things. I took on the role of his accountant, nurse, housekeeper, chauffeur, secretary, public relations person, security guard, and whatever else he needed. It was my job to make sure our finances remained intact. I coordinated his visitors. When people would call and ask him about visiting, he would say, "Talk to my wife." It was my responsibility to guard him from anyone who was coughing, sneezing, and to make sure visitors washed their hands.

We spend countless hours together compelling us to know each other in ways that we would have never otherwise known. But our relationship was no longer balanced. What started out as a partnership in fighting this illness has turned into two weary individuals who are just struggling to survive. Some well-wishers in an attempt to offer encouragement will say, "God is going to bless you for all you do for your husband." While I appreciated the kind words, it did not make the challenges I was facing any less overwhelming. Was there something that God wanted me to glean from this situation? In an effort to avoid feeling discouragement, my remedy was not to focus on the negative aspect of what we were experiencing but to immerse myself in what needed to be done.

My husband has a strong personality, and he likes things done a certain way. I also have a strong personality, and I feel I know best how to take care of him. After all, I have many years as a nurse on my résumé. One thing I have learned in the process is that the more I insist, the harder he resists. Because of the frequent opposition that I have faced in caring for him, the conflicts have resulted in some cases of me feeling apathy and numbness. I have to pray often asking God to help me to be content and show forth His love during this time. It does not matter how disagreeable my husband is I must give an account to God for how I respond to him, and as his wife who vowed to love him until death parts us, I am committed to seeing this season of our lives through to the end. My desire is not just one of wanting to finish, but I want to finish strong in a way that honors my husband and brings glory to God.

It is difficult to avoid negative thoughts when you are surrounded by negative talk daily. With the frequent complaints, it would be easy to develop a doomsday mentality. When I refuse to participate in the pity party, he sometimes perceives it as being uncaring. It is not that I am uncaring; it is that I must protect my spirit. My constant dilemma is to find ways to show that I care without sacrificing my joy.

I remember my husband commenting numerous times that he would not live to see our oldest daughter graduate high school, and I think he really believed that he would not. Well, he has seen her graduate high school, college, and graduate school. Obeying his physician's orders that he was prohibited from flying, we took a seven-day road trip to see her walk across the stage to receive her graduate degree from Miami University in Ohio. The graduation was outside, and the weather was cold and damp on that day. But we wrapped ourselves in blankets to see what he had professed he would never live to see. What a blessing it was to witness God's plan for his life. Many times, the way we feel physically will cause us to speak lies over our own lives. God is in control and we must learn to rest in Him. It is in Him we find contentment.

I often feel like I am fighting a losing battle trying to combat the negative talk. The search for contentment is ongoing as things change. Finding contentment while remaining hopeful is the key. It can be difficult for those suffering long-term illnesses to remain positive. It can also be difficult for the caregiver to constantly be the one who provides continual encouragement when it is being resisted on every side. The caregiver becomes an empty vessel after pouring out much.

Finding a place of contentment for yourself as a caregiver while trying to help your loved one be content can be perplexing. When the caregiver comes to a place of peace and the one you care for is restless, the compassion you feel for your loved one can take you out of your place of contentment. Often when my husband is in the hospital and I go home at night to rest, it is only to receive a call regarding his dissatisfaction with a member of the nursing staff. I then find myself creeping out of my place of peace and contentment.

The job of the caregiver is 24/7. Even when your loved one is in the hospital, you are still the point of contact that the medical staff relies on. I have received many calls from my husband because he did not get what he ordered for breakfast or in some cases no breakfast. Calls because his call light has been on longer than it should and no one has come to attend to his needs. It hurts my heart to know that he is unhappy, but as a caregiver I must take time to nourish myself. In those times of frustration for him which could lead to frustration for me, I must let go which is not easy. I have the personality of a fixer so my first instinct is I have to fix this. I must remind myself that there are things that I cannot fix. My obligation is to address the issues with the appropriate personnel and trust them to do their job. It is then I must pray and release it to God knowing that Scott and his present situation is in God's hands. Just as God will never leave me, He will never leave him. We both must learn to be content ultimately releasing it all to our Heavenly Father who has all power in His hands. God is still working on us.

Pray asking God to help you to learn how to be content with your current situation.
Use your accompanying journal to write what you are feeling after you have prayed.

Heart of Faith

"Be on your guard; stand firm in the faith; be courageous; be strong" (1 Corinthians 16:13).

Faith is trust and total reliance on the Word of God. Faith comes from hearing God's Word. Once we hear the Word, we can trust what God has said will come to pass. Our faith is not in things or people, but our faith is in God and what His Word says about our situation. Others may voice their opinions or suggestions regarding our condition, but we must trust what God has said in His Word concerning us.

While it is true, we will experience some difficult periods in this life, God is still the governor. He knows all there is to know about us. He orders our steps, and we must trust that He knows which path we should take. Life has its trials and share of disappointments, but God, our Creator, has placed in each of us what we will need to win the fight.

In our darkest moments, the opportunity for our faith to be strengthened is displayed. Maintaining a level of faith when life seems frenzied can be difficult. It is in our weakness that He is strong. Our faith remains firm because our faith is in a never-changing God. We can lean on Him when we are shaky because He is always solid.

It is in life's storms that we gain an understanding of God's great love. If there were no storms, how would we ever experience the deliverance of an almighty God?

The faith of the caregiver is often tested by the negative health reports, the seemingly inexhaustible complaints, and simply watching the person you care for struggle day after day. When will it end? When will the pain cease? To see your loved one deteriorate before your eyes can be disheartening. My husband has lost nearly one hundred and thirty pounds and his body has become weak and frail. His firm thick calves are a thing of the past. He is constantly in pain and we have yet to find a medication that relieves his pain. He is frequently in and out of the hospital plus having many doctors' visits. We are just trying to find someone who can help ease his pain.

Caring for a loved one is a constant reminder of suffering and pain. It is one's faith in God that keeps the believer focused and motivated. During an illness, your loved one may want to give up. Caregivers who maintain a firm faith can be an inspiration to the ones for whom they care for. When caregivers struggle with doubts, they usually will not verbalize them because if they do, then who will encourage the distressed loved one? Again, it could cause guilt.

So much is expected of the caregiver. We are expected to care for our loved ones physically, emotionally, and spiritually. This is a difficult place to be the constant cheerleader. Who cheers the caregiver? As caregivers, we empty so much of ourselves into our loved ones, but who restores us? It can be challenging to stay positive and stand strong.

When does the caregiver have an opportunity to cry? Many caregivers will not allow their true emotions to be exposed. They bottle their feeling as a means of protection against experiencing the hurt and pain. Other caregivers may become depressed and experience hopelessness. But in our times of anguish, God is always there to provide comfort and relief. Many times, He shows up in the form of a friend or family member. Sometimes it can be a telephone call from someone who cares and asks, "Do you need anything?" But there are those times when no one calls or shows up, and I have had to cry out to God for assistance.

I am confident it has been my faith that has carried me. Without a firm faith I would not have made it this far. During my moments of despair, God has always been faithful to send a reminder that He remembers me through His Word. There are moments when my anguish is so great that I feel as if God has left me, but it is my faith in Him that reminds me He is still there.

Faith can be tested by a negative doctor or hospital reports. On more than one occasion I would have to remove myself from the hospital room to avoid hearing the reports. When you visit doctor after doctor and get no concrete answers, it can sow seeds of doubt. And when you do not see the manifestation of what you have prayed for, it can be difficult to remain positive. When the seeds of doubt are sown, the negative thoughts and talk acts as water for the negative seeds. Negativity causes the seeds of doubt to flourish and grow. It can be a daily struggle for many caregivers, including me, to maintain a continual firm faith.

The Scripture teaches that when we do not ask in faith but in doubt, we will not receive anything from God. But we must ask in faith without any doubt. "But when you ask, you must believe and not doubt, because the one who doubts is like a wave of the sea, blown and tossed by the wind. That person should not expect to receive anything from the Lord. Such a person is double-minded and unstable in all they do." James 1: 6-8. If we want to receive answers to our prayers, we must ask in faith. Our faith must be firm, not skeptical.

In January 2013, my husband was admitted to the hospital with a fever. He told me he was coughing up blood-tinged mucus. I didn't see any mucus, and from what I could tell, nothing really had changed. He had been complaining for a day or two prior to my calling the doctor. A CAT scan of his chest showed a large opaque area in one of his lungs. The doctors began to speculate as to what it might be. Some thought tumor, others thought tuberculosis, and some just didn't know what to say. As a precaution, he was placed in an isolation room.

With each report, I became more anxious. I was already dealing with the remorse of not bringing him to the hospital earlier. He had been coughing for a few days, and I thought the blood-tinged sputum may have resulted from strenuous coughing combined with the dryness of the heat in the house. He didn't feel warm, so it never occurred to me to check his temperature. As a former nurse though, I should have.

With so many complaints over the years, I had learned not to panic. Maybe I had become immune to his constant complaints. I had learned to look for recurring signs of his autoimmune disease, or more definitive changes in his condition. As long as he was eating and moving about I thought he was fine.

I learned a valuable lesson from this episode. When caring for a person with an autoimmune disease, any abnormal symptom needs to be addressed. Most new symptoms can be related to the immune system in some way. Any new symptom the immune-suppressed person experiences may be due to their weakened immune system and needs to be investigated.

I was focused on the autoimmune disease and knew the signs of a flare-up would be more intense pain and paralysis. But the part I overlooked was that with the autoimmune disease, he was more susceptible to infections. It's hard, but caregivers must be observant and on-guard for many things.

During this particular hospitalization, I was dealing with the news that he might have tuberculosis. I did not feel comfortable sharing this information with anyone because tuberculosis is contagious. I was afraid that our daughters, who had been home from college for Christmas break, could have been exposed. He had gone to church a few Sundays before, and anyone who had been in contact with him could have been exposed. What if I had been exposed? I have a germ phobia anyway and things like this will set me on edge. I was prepared to deal with all of his illness, but when it came to his being contagious, I almost panicked. With these thoughts coursing through my brain, I felt as if it was about to explode. The doctors entered his room one behind the other with speculations of diagnosis, prognosis, and treatment plans.

Finally, I had to say to his doctor, "I prefer to not hear all the maybes, tell me what you know when you know for sure." Although I understood that physicians like to give you the worst-case scenario and they like to keep you informed, sometimes I think they talk to you about the most horrible possibilities so you won't come back and accuse them of not telling you something. I took periodic walks throughout the day while I was at the hospital just to clear my head. I didn't want to hear anymore theories, just the facts. Sometimes you have to close the mouth of the negative speaker. In doing so, this helped to calm the negative thoughts that were forming in my head.

Over the years, I have been accused of being in denial regarding his condition. I have never been in denial; I simply do not want my faith to waver. To keep my faith strong, I have had to be careful who and what I allowed in my ear.

My advice to caregivers is when your faith seems to waver, reaffirm what you know to be true about God. Read the Word to see what the Scripture teaches us about who He is. The Word of God teaches that He is a healer of all manner of diseases. Tuberculosis was not too hard for God.

When we do not see the manifestation of the promises in our own lives, it doesn't mean that God is not able. I made the decision to believe the Word knowing that God knew the situation we were in. I had to believe He was able to bring us out and that He would provide whatever we needed during this time. Trying to process it all in my mind overwhelmed me. I had to trust God and stand firm on my faith in Him knowing that He was able.

God did provide a physician, a man of faith, with a calming demeanor, just when I needed it. Ruling out the tuberculosis took some time. It was a process of elimination and through it all my husband remained in isolation. During this time, I was his only visitor. When people inquired, I would say, "He's in isolation and cannot have visitors," but I did not say the reason he was in isolation. I did not want to ignite fear in others and put that diagnosis of tuberculosis into the atmosphere.

To remain strong in your faith, it is essential that caregivers surround themselves with people who have firm faith. The caregiver's plate is often full and is never just dealing with one situation. While handling one thing, life goes on and other things happen. Everything keeps moving, and you may have to deal with other crises while dealing with a crisis with the one you care for. For example, I am still a mother of two daughters who were both in college at the time. I had to assist them in managing challenges that came up in their lives while dealing with my sick husband. At times I felt like a single parent. I salute single moms and all they accomplish; it can be a difficult journey raising children alone.

Often when encounters came, I had to face them alone and felt some anguish. In my mind, I knew my husband did not ask to be ill, but I also did not ask to have to manage and run our household on my own. I had to pray and guard against bitterness. I realized that

God had already equipped me with everything I would need to fulfill my assignment both as a mother and a caregiver to my husband. I would have to activate my faith like never before. God did place the right people around me to assist me during this season of my life and for that I am eternally grateful.

My mother was a great encouragement to me even while dealing with her own illness. When she was diagnosed with cancer and underwent chemotherapy, I would speak to her on the phone and visit her when I could, but I was unable to be with her toward the end. The caregiver is constantly juggling life's events, some good and some bad.

I remember getting the call that my mother had transitioned; I was driving carpool at six-thirty in the morning with six high school students in the car. I quickly told my brother I would call him back after I dropped off the students. I had planned a trip to visit her the next day because on that day my husband had a doctor's appointment and I needed to accompany him. My delay in visiting her meant that I would never see my mother again on this side of heaven. Her death was somewhat expected but unanticipated at that moment. Our family had just made plans by phone the night before for her continued care. I had no control in the situation but God did. He made sure that everyone was being cared for and I understand He has a purpose for everything, but it still hurt. I missed both of my mother and father's passing. I choose to trust God in this.

Other responsibilities of life continue when you become a caregiver. If you are a parent, you are still a parent. For many, they must still maintain a career to provide for the family. I did not stop being a mother or a daughter when I became my husband's caregiver.

Caregivers miss out on much of the routines of life when they become consumed by their role as a caregiver. It is easy to become overwhelmed with the illness that has touched your family. In the process, you neglect other things that require your attention. At the time the illness is all that matters, but then you look back and realize what you neglected mattered as well. I have missed visits with family and friends, birthday celebrations, and other important days because of my duties as a caregiver. I had planned to celebrate my fiftieth birthday in a big way. When that day arrived, my husband was a little over one-month post-transplant. Any plans I had took a backseat to my responsibilities as a caregiver.

In the pursuit to accomplish it all, life can become very stressful. Caregivers will not be able to do it all. We must rely on our firm faith in God to sustain us. As we trust in God and not ourselves we will not become overwhelmed. God is strong, and He is able to support us so that we do not fall under the pressure of caregiving.

When I drove to North Carolina, the day after my mother passed, I went directly from Florida to the funeral home to assist with the arrangements. It still amazes me that we were able to pull everything together so quickly, but God strengthened us as a family to do what needed to be done. After my mother's service, we gathered to clean out the senior apartment she had been living in, and I headed back to Tampa but ended up spending the night four hours from home. I needed a moment just to regroup and pull my thoughts together. I knew that once I got home, my caregiving duties would resume, and I just needed some time to refocus my mind. After a nice dinner at the hotel restaurant and good night phone calls, I turned in for a good night's rest.

The next morning, I was on the road early heading home because I was the caregiver for my husband and I had to get back to take care of him. It was good to take that time to refuel before returning home, both for him and me.

Heart of Faith

My journey as a caregiver has not gone without the testing of my faith. There have been times I felt like giving up and throwing in the towel, but I am thankful that God never gave up on me. Some days I would wake up and think, "I just won't go to the hospital today." But I knew my husband would call if I didn't show up by a certain time. I realized that as long as my faith was in God, I could do all things through Him. So with that in mind, I would head out the door to the hospital.

I try not to dwell too long on the bad times because I understand that the joy of the Lord is my strength. Negative thoughts and negative talk can lead to depression. A thankful heart can cause you to feel empowered and strong. In those times when my faith is weak, I turn to God's Word and the listening ear of a confidant. Finding someone you can trust and share with will be helpful on your caregiver's journey. It can be hard for a spouse to share intimate details about the other with an outsider. But having a friend or counselor who you can share with and know that that person will still love you and your spouse can be a lifesaver. You will not be able to talk to everyone, but chose someone who you can confide in.

As believers and caregivers, we have to stand on the truth of God's Word. It is in His Word that we find security and comfort. Even though my husband's body is feeble, and I have become the physically strong one, I can always go to God for safety. It is in Him one will find strength for the journey. He is a soft place we can always fall and a firm place we can always stand. We must know without a doubt that God holds our lives in His hand. Our faith is planted in Him and in His Word. Situations change, people change, but the Word of God remains stable. That is where we can stand and know that we will not fall.

He is the same yesterday, today, and forever. He does not change. When things are changing all around us, He is our solid rock. He does not vacillate in times of uncertainty. I have had to be the strong one for my husband and our children. My strength comes from God because on my own I would fall every time. Yes, I have my moments when I feel like my world is crashing around me. But then I quickly remember where I stand. On Christ the solid rock is where my faith is firmly planted.

When asked what has been of most help to me as a caregiver, the answer is my faith in God. Because He is sovereign and I love Him, I have to believe that everything is working for my good. Apostle Paul writes in Romans 8:28, "And we know that in all things God works for the good of those who love him, who have been called according to his purpose." The reference of *all things* is the suffering of this present world. The situations will work together in collaboration for my good. Every suffering moment that I experience will somehow assist me in being conformed to the image of Christ. No matter what difficulties I am facing in my life I must trust and rely on God. My faith must remain firm, unshakable, and unmovable. Then I am able to stand.

Pray asking God to increase your faith.
Use your accompanying journal to write what you are feeling after you have prayed.

Forgiving Heart

"For if you forgive other people when they sin against you, your heavenly Father will also forgive you. But if you do not forgive others their sins, your Father will not forgive your sins" (Matthew 6:14-15).

Conflict between a caregiver and the person cared for can be perplexing to navigate. When one is ill, you no longer have an even playing field. The person who is sick may lash out and the caregivers may feel that they have no choice other than to accept what has been said or done. Perhaps the pain made him do it. Maybe it's the medication that alters his mood. We rationalize and choose not to believe that anyone could be so unkind especially someone we care for.

Not wanting to be perceived as "mean," the caregiver keeps quiet and accepts responsibility for another person's behavior. But what does the caregiver do with all of the negative emotions that have been suppressed. Surely some of it is pain, but could some of it be just the negative feeling of the person you are caring for? Ask yourself if this is the way the person behaved prior to the illness. Relationships have conflict, this we know. Determining how much of the conflict is related to the illness and how much is just life experiences can be confusing.

If the negative attitude is related to the illness, it does not make the words any less painful to hear. The fact that the caregiver cannot freely express and receive clear feedback is disheartening. Friends may advise you to avoid the drama, but that is easier said than done.

If you have never experienced caring for a sick spouse, then it will be difficult for you to understand what I am saying. Not being drawn into the drama is difficult to do when the drama keeps coming day after day.

Other well-wishers are quick to point out that we should remember our loved one the way they were before they got sick. Honestly, my husband has been ill since June 2008 and sometimes it is hard for me to remember the kind of person he was before he became ill. His illness has become a part of our lives. Sometimes, I think it is all I know. As we age, we grow and our interest change. The kinds of things we dealt with years ago are different now. When dealing with certain situations that come up in our home, I cannot say how he would have responded before he was ill. I only know how he relates to certain things as an unhealthy person.

Our daughters were in middle and high school when he first got sick. Now when confronted with an issue relating to adult daughters, I cannot imagine how he would have responded as a healthy father. I have been the one to do the college drop-offs and pick-ups, the moving in and out of dorms and apartments, and deal with the emergencies that have come up over the past years. Some of which I was unable to share with him because of his fragile condition. I have had to bear much in silence.

There are times I feel like I am on an emotional rollercoaster. When my husband's condition prevents him from being a part of things, I take the lead so that everything will be taken care of. Because his condition fluctuates there may be times when he is able to take a more active role in the management of our home. When he feels better, he wants to not just move back into position, but he wants to modify what I have done. This would be great if his health would allow him to stay in that position. Often his upward swing is short-lived, and once again I have to shift my position. Living life like this can be unsettling and unsatisfying. Making decisions that you think are best for the family then having someone undo your hard work only to leave you to deal with the fall-out as their condition deteriorates again. His heart is in the right place, but his body will not cooperate. And while I understand his predicament, it does not make the frequent transitioning any less stressful for me.

Since his illness, I am left to make the decisions concerning our home and our family, including the management of the finances. In addition to having single parent responsibilities, I still have the responsibility of being a caregiver. It seems that my status is married without the benefits of the partnership of marriage, and yet single without the freedom of being carefree.

The caregiver is overwhelmed with the myriad of emotions they experience. The constant ups and downs can create anxiety. There is also the constant struggle to be flexible and go with the flow, which can also produce apprehension. The caregiver tries to do all of these things while retaining some stability. The caregiver may experience anger, guilt, and resentment not comprehending why.

Emotions are complex and not always understood. The feelings are of course unreasonable; who can be angry because someone is ill? The anger is not because of the illness; it is anger caused by the results of the illness. A chronic illness brings with it many unwelcome changes. Sometimes it is difficult to separate the experienced emotions brought on by the disease from the person who has the disease.

I am often told that I am a very calm person. But even calm people like me can struggle with the feelings of annoyance, blame, and apathy. The numbness is a defense tool that helps me to handle everything that has happened. It is a coping mechanism, allowing me to hide behind the emotion and not confront the issue. This is not good, but it is safe and comfortable. However, we all know that things will have to be dealt with sooner or later.

Practicing forgiveness becomes a daily chore. In life when people hurt us, we forgive them and set boundaries to avoid being hurt again. The restrictions we put on our relationship with a person can be lifesaving. In many cases, it saves the relationship by redefining it, and it saves our sanity in some cases. But how do you put restrictions on the relationship with the person you are caring for? When you express your concerns and they seem not to be heard?

The ill family member may apologize over and over, only to repeat the offence. To forgive, it is not easy, but it is imperative that the caregiver be ready to forgive. Remember, forgiveness is really more about you than the other person. Holding unresolved issues can be damaging to the body and to the spirit. It can be difficult when you are caring for someone who repetitively debates and opposes you on every decision or becomes defensive when questioned about a decision.

When a person feels that control has been taken away, they lash out to control whatever they can. Usually, the caregiver receives the impact of the frustrations expressed by the loved one who is ill. The caregivers may not be able to express their concerns to the person they are caring for. This person is facing strong conflict trying to cope with the illness, and many times, will not be thinking rationally. Therefore, the caregiver will need to release it to God.

Learn to pray about everything and allow God to carry the load. Cast your cares on Him. The word cast means to place upon. If you have placed it on God, then it cannot be on you and God at the same time. God is able to bear what we cannot bear.

There are times when I am not feeling well physically and my husband will express a physical symptom he is feeling. In my mind I just want to cry out, "If you knew how bad I felt, you would not complain to me." But when a person is experiencing chronic pain and discomfort, it becomes very difficult for them to recognize and respond to the needs of another person. Complaining as the caregiver about my affliction somehow seems selfish. After all, he is the one with the incurable disease.

Some days I did not feel like driving and sitting through long doctor appointments. I struggled to get him where he needed to be in spite of how I was feeling physically. Being the only driver in the house has its challenges. One is, to get home and realize you need something and have to go back out after being out all day. I did not feel like spending all day and night at the hospital because he did not want me to go home. There were times when I stayed at the hospital all day and way into the night. If I had known I had to stay so late into the night, I would not have come up so early in the morning. But who does the caregiver complain to?

My hesitancy in complaining was twofold. It had to do with my husband's illness and the fact that many caregivers have to work outside of the home and take care of a loved one. My full-time job was caring for my husband and I should be thankful. After all, it was because of my husband that I had been afforded the opportunity to be a stay-at-home mom all of those years. I realized that many caregivers work all day and come home to take care of a loved one. What if I had to take care of him and work a full-time job? As rational as these points were, it did not dismiss the feelings of weariness I experienced.

Finally, I had to reconcile that this was my journey and it could not be compared to anyone else's. What I was feeling were my feelings and I could not deny them. Yes, some caregivers have additional responsibilities outside of the home, but in some cases that can be a blessing. They have something else to focus on for part of the day. For others like me, it is constant; no outside full-time employment providing an outlet. Either way, caregiving is a tough job.

I would caution caregivers not to take on too much outside of the home if possible. When it comes to volunteering our time, many women have difficulty saying no. Other people will not understand the all-encompassing role of caregiving and may ask you to work on other projects. Whether it be work, community, or church you will need to step away from some things.

As caregiver for my husband, I do not have the privilege of having him run to the store or pick something up on his way home like he once did. I have to do it all now. When I am sick and my doctors tells me that I need to rest, that's a good idea but not probable. Family and friends are often telling the caregiver to get rest. Caregivers do not neglect rest on purpose. Many times, their duties as a caregiver prevent them from getting proper rest.

I am the caregiver; it is my job to take care of him. But who takes care of the caregivers? The caregiver is overlooked many times. When the patient is in the hospital, many will want to visit the patient. The caregiver will need visitors too. Just having someone come and sit with the caregiver without even going in the patient's room can be valuable.

The heart of the caregiver is to do a good job at what they do. They want to show love in all that they do, but sometimes it can be a challenge. What starts off as a gesture done out of love from the caregiver when confronted with dislike from the patient can convert to a gesture done out of obligation.

Learning to release the negative emotions is essential. Seek the counsel of a friend or professional. The person you are caring for may not have the capacity to reach out to you. The ill person is overwhelmed with their illness and in some cases consumed. My husband researches his illness on the internet and he is quite informed, in some cases more than his physicians. Being knowledgeable is good, but even in that there must be balance.

I try not to focus too much on my husband's illness because it then becomes a reminder to me of the things we are no longer able to do. Dwelling on what you gave up or missed out on as a caregiver can result in bitterness and other negative attitudes. Remember to not let undesirable attitudes or anger sneak in. Learn to practice daily forgiveness. Be quick to forgive, do not hold onto things. Do not allow negativity to linger in your thoughts, mind, or heart. Allowing things to fester can lead to bitterness. Be willing to forgive quickly and move on lest rage and cynicism sets in.

We are not to keep count of deeds done to us, but we must always be willing to forgive. When we can forgive, we are allowing God to take care of the matter. We do not hold offense and hatred toward those who have hurt us. Forgiveness is not easy under any circumstances especially when you are still in the battle. But make forgiveness a daily commitment as a caregiver. As a caregiver, I have had to ask for forgiveness as well as give forgiveness.

There will be those who are judgmental of how you handle things. They will look at you and try to offer suggestions as to what you should do and how you should behave. Forgive them. It's so much easier that way.

It is easy for onlookers to label you as a caregiver. Others will not understand all you do as a caregiver. They only see the public side but do not see what goes on behind the scenes. On-lookers may only see your smile, not your tears. Many times when I would go places, no one really knows what it took for me to just get there. People only see the glory but they do not know your story. They cannot appreciate the frustration a caregiver experiences daily. The struggle of dealing with a noncompliant patient may not be appreciated by someone who has never had that experience. Those on the outside will not know you have offered to help, but your help was rejected repeatedly.

As the caregiver, you are endeavoring to allow your loved one to maintain a level of independence. You are attempting to relate to them as a human being in an effort to help them to maintain a level of dignity. This requires great patience and a willingness to forgive when your efforts are rejected.

I remember being in the doctor's office one day with my husband and he dropped his cane. I was sitting on the other side of the waiting room and the lady sitting closest to him picked it up for him. When we got home, he inquired as to why I did not help him when he dropped his cane. All I could think of was the number of times I have reached to pick up things he has dropped to hear him say "I got it" or "I can do it myself." Truly the life of a caregiver is an emotional rollercoaster, never knowing when or what is the correct thing to do.

Caregivers know the behind the scene conflicts they encounter and they cannot allow the negative feelings of others to influence them. The observer only sees that your loved one appears to need help and you are not offering. What they do not understand is the complexity of the situation. One day your loved one may want independence and the next they may desire assistance. Harsh judgement of caregivers can be unfair based purely on ignorance of the gravity of the situation.

It is human nature for people to criticize what they do not understand. Learn to forgive them and do not hold it against them. Remember that when Jesus was on the cross, He said, "Father, forgive them; for they know not what they do" (Luke 23:34 KJV). They really do not have a clue as to what your life is like. If they have never walked in your shoes, then they cannot begin to understand your plight. Many times, you are stuck between allowing your loved one independence and literally trying to make it through the day with your sanity intact.

Forgiving Heart

My husband will ask for forgiveness when things come to his mind. Many of the things he brings up I do not remember. Interestingly enough, the things I remember he does not. It has almost become a routine with him to apologize for things that have happened over the years. I guess it is his way of clearing his conscience, so I listen and accept his apology.

Holding unresolved issues inside will be harmful to you. This I know from experience. I went through the early years of our marriage holding onto things. I had to learn what most people already knew that you cannot change a person. For years, I wanted my husband to be more available to me, to spend time together doing things that we enjoyed. Well, I now have his attention twenty-four hours a day, but not the way I wanted it. Maybe God does have a sense of humor.

I am thankful to God that I have been able to forgive and keep moving forward focusing on the assignment at hand. The road as his caregiver is not easy but I know that God will carry me through. He has proven that so many times.

Practicing frequent forgiveness will free your heart and mind to receive all that God has for you. What He has is perfect.

Pray acknowledging all unresolved disputes and ask for forgiveness.
Use your accompanying journal to write what you are feeling after you have prayed.

See Me Hear Me Know Me

Heart to Do Good

"Finally, brothers and sisters, whatever is true, whatever is noble, whatever is right, whatever is pure, whatever is lovely, whatever is admirable—if anything is excellent or praiseworthy—think about such things" (Philippians 4:8).

Mark 10:18 reads, "Why do you call me good?" Jesus answered. "No one is good—except God alone." God is the only one with a right to deity. Caregivers can establish goodness in their lives which can be seen in how they treat the one they care for and others.

The word good speaks of being pleasant, agreeable, joyful, and happy. When caring for a loved one, these qualities can brighten the day of both the caregiver and the patient. The circumstances of life may be far from good but we can remain pleasant, agreeable, joyful, and happy. Understanding that Jesus is the source of all good things is the foundation on which we stand. James 1:17, "Every good and perfect gift is from above, coming down from the Father of the heavenly lights, who does not change like shifting shadows." Again we see pleasant, agreeable, joyful, and happy. Other words that speak to good in this Scripture are excellent, distinguished, upright, honorable, and of good constitution or nature.

These are all words that bring a smile to your face. On the days you do not feel like smiling as a caregiver, think of goodness. Think of all the good things in your life. Think about the people who demonstrate God's goodness that are in your life. They are able to stand with you as a caregiver because the goodness of God shines through them. Think about how good God has been and continues to be.

Goodness is one of the characteristics of God as well as an explanation of His very essence. God, by nature, is essentially good as Psalm 34:8 reads, "Taste and see that the LORD is good; blessed is the one who takes refuge in him." He is the base of goodness and of everything good. His goodness does not come from any other source. He is the source. But the goodness that we display comes as a result of God living in us.

There are many days when I leave the house with my only intention being to walk outside just to be among nature. God's creation, seeing the trees, the birds, the flowers, the grass and the other plants remind me of the goodness of God. He takes care of the earth, the trees and plants. Nature does not worry like man because God provides what is needed. If our good God provides what is needed to sustain life for nature, surely He will provide for us. Being among nature gives assurance that God has and will continue to provide all that we have need of. Seeing the array of His goodness in the earth brings joy and hope. Even on the hardest days, we can trust God to refresh us.

As a caregiver, there are numerous days when I walk and listen to music. Yes, I enjoy the exercise benefits of walking, but some days it is simply to relax my mind. My walks are meant to experience the goodness of God. While I am walking, I meditate on His goodness. I thank Him for all the good things He has done for me and those around me. It is precious time that I enjoy in His presence.

I find that when I have stepped away from my current status of caregiver, just for a few moments, my mind is renewed. I can once again see joy in the small things in life. The life of a caregiver is filled with doing things for others. It is very important for caregivers to take some time away for themselves. The caregiver's free time will be limited, but it is important to schedule some getaway time for themselves. Perhaps they will not be able to do some of the fun things they once did. They may not have the time or the resources to go on vacation, but take a walk, smell the flowers. This refreshment will help the caregiver.

Fortunately, I live in Florida, so I can enjoy the outdoors year-round. If you live in places where the weather doesn't cooperate, look out the window. Look at the sky, read books that take you to fun places. As a little girl, I remember traveling through the pages of books. Reading would allow me to go places in my mind that I could only dream of traveling to one day.

If you are a caregiver who is unable to go for walks, try watching television shows about nature and marvel at the goodness of God. I had one of the most relaxing experiences in the hospital chapel recently. The chapel had a rotating video on the entire front wall of scenes from nature. I experienced the valleys and the mountains. I spent time watching and listening to the waters. There were also videos of the fields with animals grazing. These soothing scenes of nature continuously rotating with soft music in the background on the chapel front wall had a relaxing effect on me. While watching a calm sea and the raging waves, although it was only a video, it brought calmness to my anxious soul. My husband was in the emergency room at the time, so I slipped away for just a few minutes to renew my spirit.

God is truly good even in the most difficult of our situations. There may be bad things happening all around, but God is still good. Just thinking of the goodness of Jesus brings a smile to my face. My current circumstance is not what I want it to be, and I have been through some tough times. But I can rejoice because God has brought me through. He did not leave me there to struggle in the chaos. He did not abandon me to figure my own way out, but He brought me out. That is the goodness of God.

When I think back on how the dynamics of our lives as a family have changed over the past years, I know it was the goodness of God that kept us. It was His goodness that provided for all of our needs. When we were in a place of lack, it was He who supplied everything we needed according to His riches in glory (Philippians 4:19).

God is good. Lamentations 3:21–26 reads, "Yet this I call to mind and therefore I have hope: Because of the Lord's great love we are not consumed, for His compassions never fail. They are new every morning; great is your faithfulness. I say to myself, 'The Lord is my portion; therefore I will wait for him.' The Lord is good to those whose hope is in him, to the one who seeks him; it is good to wait quietly for the salvation of the Lord."

We see the goodness of God every day. His goodness is in the people God places in our lives to assist us. We even see the hand of His goodness in negative situations. His mercies are new every morning.

Good things may not always show up as happy experiences. Sometimes good can come concealed as misfortune or adversity, but God can use the difficult times of our lives to show us His goodness. It is God's goodness that keeps us focused on Him when we are drowning in despair. It has been God's goodness in my life that would not let me go even when I wanted to escape.

Goodness is who He is. People can have good qualities or do good deeds, but goodness is not in our character by nature. In fact, the Scripture teaches that we were born with a sinful nature. Psalm 51:5 reads, "Surely I was sinful at birth, sinful from the time my mother conceived me." Our goodness comes from God. As a caregiver, there have been times that my flesh wanted to rise up and say, "Enough." When you do all you can and no one is satisfied, what do you do? God desires that we show goodness through our lives and to others in our lives. As a caregiver, you may not always show the goodness that you desire to show.

On those difficult days when you miss it, try again to express the characteristics of the good God that we serve. You may have to walk away from the situation as not to allow your good intentions to be crushed. Slip away and pray. God is a present help in the time of trouble.

Just as God's goodness is evident in all that He created, His goodness must be evident in all that we do. Since it does not come naturally to us, we must work on demonstrating goodness. There is nothing we can do to earn God's goodness. It is available to us regardless of our position in life, and even though we are not worthy of it, God is still good to us. Psalm 145:9 reads, "The LORD is good to all; he has compassion on all he has made."

There may be days as a caregiver when you feel like the person for whom you are caring doesn't deserve a kind word because of how they treat you. Remember, you represent the good God that you serve, so ask yourself, "How would Jesus respond?"

God's goodness is intentional and we must be intentional about showing His goodness to others. There are days I have to seek the face of God asking Him to help me to show His goodness as I care for my husband. There are days that my husband does not want to eat and trying to convince him is exhausting. But when I think of God's goodness, it compels me to ask him again. Maybe he will say yes this time. Sometimes I have to leave the room and come back in a few minutes to start all over again.

We must understand that just as our God is a good God, His purpose for us is good. Jeremiah 29:11 reads, "For I know the plans I have for you," declares the Lord, "plans to prosper you and not to harm you, plans to give you hope and a future." Just as we desire good things for our children, God desires good things for us. The situation you are in as a caregiver may not be a good situation, but if our good God is there with us than we will be able to prevail.

God will always be good. His character does not change. He will continue to be the maker of all things good and we can be assured that He will provide good things for us according to His perfect plan. When we love God, even when the situation is not good, God is working it out for our good. I have learned so much about love and sacrifice over the past years. The lessons I have learned will assist me in helping others.

I am thankful for the goodness of God in my life during my journey as a caregiver. We can see evidence of this all around us in how He provides for our needs. He provides opportunities for us, opens the right doors, and touches the heart of people to be a blessing to us. I do not know how He does it, but I am grateful.

The goodness of God is the central part of our beings as Christians. If He was not a good God, He would not have given His Son to die for our sins. Everything He does is in some form working for our good. We may not see it right away and many times we lack understanding, but we know that God is good.

Because God is good, we can practice goodness by showing it to others because He lives in us. In an effort to do what I believe is best for my husband, my actions at times may seem harsh, but God sees my heart. My husband accuses me of being too tough, but the moment he needs an advocate, he relies on my toughness to accomplish the desired outcome. "It's okay to be tough with everyone else just do not be tough with me," is what he is really saying.

My prayer is to demonstrate the goodness of God in all I do. I do not want to have any regrets. I want my ways to please the Lord. If God should call my husband home before he calls me, I want to know that I have done everything I could to make his days pleasant. I want to show goodness in my actions not simply with words. Even if my husband gets frustrated with me in the process, I need to do what pleases God. Even if the good deeds I do are not reciprocated, I must continue to allow the goodness of God to be demonstrated through me to him.

As caregivers, our aim should be to show the goodness of God to the ones we care for daily. The gift we give to our loved ones is caring. Some days I want a vacation from caring because I feel drained and empty. It is as though I have nothing left to give. Many times, when caregivers are constantly giving out and nothing is being returned, emotional exhaustion will set in. But even in those times, our good God gives the strength needed to continue the journey.

It is important that the caregivers know their value. The fact that you are healthy is not a punishment just as the fact that your loved one is ill is not a punishment. The place God has you at this time may be difficult to understand. You may have questions but know that He is with you and He wants His goodness to shine in all you do.

Spread the *Son* shine in the lives of those you care for. The goodness of Jesus is a good medication for whatever troubles us and should be freely shared with all. With love and kindness, He drew us to Himself and that same love and kindness will draw others to Him. The heart of a caregiver is a heart seeking to share the same goodness that one has received from the Father.

See Me Hear Me Know Me

Pray asking God to help you to see all the good that He has put in front of you.

Use your accompanying journal to write what you are feeling after you have prayed.

Hopeful Heart

"Praise be to the God and Father of our Lord Jesus Christ! In his great mercy he has given us new birth into a living hope through the resurrection of Jesus Christ from the dead, and into an inheritance that can never perish, spoil or fade. This inheritance is kept in heaven for you, who through faith are shielded by God's power until the coming of the salvation that is ready to be revealed in the last time.
In all this you greatly rejoice, though now for a little while you may have had to suffer grief in all kinds of trials" (1 Peter 1:3-6).

Hope speaks of having a desire, living in a state of anticipation and expectancy. My first few years as a caregiver were spent with the expectancy that Scott would be completely healed and everything would return to normal. I went to sleep each night thinking, "Tomorrow will be different." Tomorrow he will be well and our lives will continue as we had planned.

Now, many years later, there are days when my greatest hope is that we both wake up in the morning. While I still believe he could be completely healed, his day-to-day needs are at the forefront of my mind. A day with less pain would be a blessing. Maybe this new doctor has an answer? Maybe my searching of articles and watching medical talk shows on television will bring us some new information and answers. I hope that maybe there will be a guest on the show with a similar condition and we can learn something new that will be helpful to Scott.

Our current status is our new normal. We have minimal expectation and fewer dreams for the future. Our greatest desire is to just maintain a stable status, which would be enough for now. I now find myself hoping we can just stay out of the hospital another day. Outpatient appointments we can do and in-house therapy is good, but no admissions, please.

The year 2015 was good for Scott; he was admitted in March and had no other admissions for the remainder of the year, but then we started January 2016 with two emergency room visits which led to him being admitted.

My husband was admitted to a medical floor and transferred the next day to a progressive care unit. The next day, he was moved to intensive care only to be transferred to a cardiac care unit at another hospital the same day. After spending two nights in the cardiac care unit, he was moved to a progressive care bed. He was then scheduled for surgery, which meant he would spend one night in the surgical intensive care unit postoperative.

What was supposed to be one night turned into three because of complications. Afterward he was moved to the medical intensive care unit. After ten days in the medical intensive care unit, he was once again transferred back to a progressive care bed on the same unit he was on before surgery. The struggle to not lose hope is a constant one with all of the medical challenges that he encountered.

I no longer hope to go on a family vacation; it is too difficult for him to travel. The enormous amount of pain he experiences from riding in the car is heartbreaking. Also, the conflict that ensues when we start to pack his durable medical equipment, which he insists he does not need although the doctors say he does, is exhausting. It has become less stressful for me to stay home and avoid confrontation. Or worse, to follow his wishes and not take any equipment and get far away from home and need something that we did not bring. So we do not do family vacations anymore.

I struggle with understanding his thought process in regards to the equipment. If there is room in the car why is there a reluctance to bring it? If we were using public transportation, I could understand limiting unnecessary items. His hesitancy to cooperate has limited our mobility, and because he does not do well alone, my travel is restricted. Over the years, I have learned that when relief is available; I need to take a few days away to gain renewed perspective.

I no longer hope to go out to dinner with him. He does not drive, so I would have to drive, choose the restaurant, and make any required plans. Most of what he eats hurts his stomach so meal time is not pleasurable. It has become easier to cook at home or to use a delivery service. Going to theater, amusement parks, sporting events, or visits with friends takes extra planning. Is their valet parking? Are there elevators? There are also concerns regarding the weather for any outdoor events. He does not do well in the heat, and the cold is too much for him.

When caring for a loved one, the majority of focus is on the present. But planning the future is still important. What do you do when your present circumstance gives you little in which to hope? Our hope must be built on something other than what we see before us. Hope must be in someone who is greater than us. Our Savior is steady; He does not vacillate. Life as we know it is uncertain at its best and in some cases falling apart. Discouragement may be all around you and cause you to feel like nothing is working out. Remember, hope is still alive. It is not in your relationships, your job, or your money. The only thing that fully satisfies is a relationship with the only true and living God. He is the solid rock. He does not change; He is unshakable, unmovable, and a firm foundation. Relationship with others can fail, jobs can be absent and money can vanish, but hope in Christ is sure.

God is the God of all comfort and strength even when our bodies ache from the physical labor of caring for a loved one. Through all the laundry, the house cleaning, the sleep deprivation, the weary bodies and mental fatigue, and the numerous appointments, God is our hope. When we are most anxious and fearful, know that God is the source of all strength. We must look past what we are experiencing today and look forward to the hope of a brighter tomorrow.

When you feel emotionally and physically frail and think that you cannot handle it anymore, God is there. He will keep your heart and mind strong in Him if you trust Him. Life may not seem fair but trust in the Lord. He has a purpose and a plan for all things. When things do not turn out the way you hope they will, you can have hope in Christ.

I do not have the ability to tell you what that plan is but God does not make mistakes, so we must concede that He knows what He is doing. Hope in Him, He will calm your apprehensions and your fears. Death may seem inevitable for our loved ones, but if their hope is in the Lord, then that is not a bad thing for those who suffer. For the Scripture promise for the believer in 2 Corinthians 5:8 reads, "We are confident, I say, and would prefer to be away from the body and at home with the Lord."

Not all caregivers experience appreciation from the ones they care for. Some never hear the words "thank you," but remember God sees all, and He knows all. He will reward you for your faithfulness in caring for your loved one.

When life seems to be crumbling all around us, we can go to our source. Jesus says to you, "Come to me, all you who are weary and burdened, and I will give you rest" (Matthew 11:28). When we feel overwhelmed and seem to have lost hope, Jesus will give us rest.

God is near to those who are broken hearted. He promises that when we cry out to Him, He will deliver us. The verb delivers means to snatch away, rescue, or to save. Our Heavenly Father does respond to our cry. Even when the situation remains unchanged, He can take us to a place of peace in Him.

It is essential that you surround yourself with positive people who can encourage you when you feel your hope dwindling. You as a caregiver need encouragement. Caregivers need others to ask how they are doing. They do not want others to feel sorry for them, but they do want others to realize that the illness has not only affected the sick family member. The entire family has been touched by the illness. We need prayer warriors who will intercede for us when we do not have the strength to pray for ourselves.

Some may ask, "How can Christians not be able to pray for themselves?" When my husband was first diagnosed with cancer and we were debating whether or not he should receive chemotherapy, I was so overwhelmed by everything that was happening and I could not focus. I thank God for the prayer warrior that fasted and prayed for us. It was the prayers of others that carried us. Even today when the pressure of a situation becomes too great, God has placed people around us who will pray for us.

Often, you do not have to tell these warriors the magnitude of the situation, but they will stand in the gap and intercede on your behalf. What a blessing to know that when your hope is diminishing, others are standing in the gap for you.

In trying to maintain hope, it sometimes gets awkward for me when people ask how my husband is doing. I really do not know how to respond. If I say he is doing well that is not an entirely true statement. But if I say he is not doing well, then it somehow appears that I am losing hope which is also not the truth. For me the best response is, "Keep him in your prayers and I will let him know you asked about him."

On occasion my husband has instructed me not to tell people he is doing well because he is not. When I asked, "What do you want me to tell them?" He responded, "Tell them to ask me." Such a response felt strange to me. I was caught between wanting people to remain hopeful while denying the facts of his illness.

My confidence in God's ability to restore remains unchanged, but we have to accept our current state. Scott is sick and I am his caregiver. That is my current circumstances, but my truth is that my hope remains in God. Apostle Paul writes in Romans 15:13, "May the God of hope fill you with all joy and peace as you trust in him, so that you may overflow with hope by the power of the Holy Spirit." The base of our hope is the God of hope. He is just as supreme today as He was in Bible days. He still answers when we cry out to Him for help. Even when my current situation appears to be hopeless, my hope can remain intact because my hope is in God.

Circumstances can evolve or regress. That is why it is important that our hope be established in the God who never changes. On our best and worst days, He is our hope. When the pain is great, and the medication does not seem to bring relief, we can still hope in the Lord. It may seem like the sky is falling in your neighborhood but God is greater than any situation you may be facing. Trust in Him; hope in Him. Stand on the solid rock that cannot be moved by wind or storm. Do not let anything destroy your hope in God.

When our faith is secure in Christ, we realize that our hope is not in the answer to the prayer. We may not receive the answer we desire when we pray. But if our lives are firmly planted in Christ, this means that our hope is in the One to whom we pray. When I

Hopeful Heart

do not see the manifestation of healing that I prayed for, my hope can remain intact because my hope is in the Healer.

If my husband never receives good health on this earth, my hope rests in the Great Physician. When we understand that our hope is in Christ even when our lives are rotated upside down, we can rest in the hope that He will be with us. He will sustain us and carry us to the finish line. We will hear our God say, "Well done."

We cannot look at our conditions. Focusing on Christ and not the situation is the key to survival. Life will always offer challenges, but if we can continue to be centered on Christ and who He is, our resolve will continue to be strong.

When you really think about it, does it really matter how you get to the finish line? If He has to carry you, it's alright because the goal is to finish the race. It is in times of the caregivers' diminishing hope that God wants to renew and reaffirm to us just who He is.

Pray asking God to renew your hope for the future and for the plans that He has for your life.

Use your accompanying journal to write what you are feeling after you have prayed.

See Me Hear Me Know Me

Kind and Loving Heart

"Be kind and compassionate to one another, forgiving each other, just as in Christ God forgave you" (Ephesians 4:32).

"And now these three remain: faith, hope and love. But the greatest of these is love" (1 Corinthians 13:13)

In the above Scripture the word kind speaks of being affectionate towards another. Whether it is a kind word, gesture, or deed, we all can agree that the world needs a little more kindness. I believe that kindness can be as effective as medication in the process of healing. When a person is experiencing pain and suffering, acts of kindness can lift their spirit.

Kindness is the value and quality of one's character. It speaks of being mild-mannered or meek. A person who demonstrates a kind and gentle spirit will be encouraging to those experiencing difficulties in life.

As a caregiver, it is important that we apply gentleness in caring for the sick. And it is also essential that the caregiver receives gentleness. Being thoughtful of others is a trait that most of us would like to show on a continual basis. But how do we handle it when our acts of kindness are met with resistance and defiance?

This can be challenging when caring for someone when that person feels as if control has been taken away. The individual who is ill may struggle to maintain control in the areas that one can, and many times the caregiver receives the impact of the ill family member's frustration.

Apostle Paul writes in 1 Corinthians 13 the characteristics describing one who loves. He explains in great detail how love demonstrates itself. To lead in love means to show love first. Even when the love is not reciprocated, we continue to show love. Our love is not based on how the other person behaves or what the other person does.

On a good day when everything lines up the way we want it to, most of us can exhibit the traits that Apostle Paul writes about. But there are those days when you did not get much sleep because your loved one was up all night. You have not had time to eat or shower. You are irritable because nothing is working out the way you planned. It is in those moments it becomes a bit more challenging to demonstrate love.

My professional background as a nurse prepared me to take care of the sick, but it's difficult when the sick person is your husband. What do you do when your offer to help is not received? When every suggestion is met with a defensive response and it feels like everything is a battle. Exhibiting the characteristics of love becomes a bit more challenging at that point. You loved the person you married but what about the person they have become?

Even though we know the characteristics of love that the apostle writes about, it can become a struggle to demonstrate them. It is difficult to be patient with a person who tests your patience. You as the caregiver may offer what you think is a gesture of love and your loved one totally rejects it. Love is patience at work.

Showing kindness is a demonstration of love. People know when you love them by the way you treat them. It is not easy to be kind to a person who is unkind to you. The excuse of pain can only be used so many times and then a person has to take responsibility for their actions. Unless the person is mentally incapacitated, they are most likely aware of their actions. Could it be that sometimes people use illness as an excuse to say and do whatever they want to do?

When you are a caregiver, you cannot just close the door when you have had enough of their treatment of you and leave your loved one alone. You as the caregiver must be involved in the decision-making process of those you care for. No matter how the person treats you, they still need a caregiver and you cannot simply walk away. But this does not mean that the caregiver should accept abuse from the ill family member. The loved one who is ill does not get a free-pass to treat people badly. It is imperative that each person, the caregiver and ill family member realize that each will be held accountable for what is done to the other. If someone is not showing you kindness, to love means that you show them kindness regardless. You may have to ask for help in dealing with tough situations. As a caregiver, you cannot allow anyone to take advantage of you or be abusive in any way. When abuse is shown toward you as the caregiver, it may be time to look at alternatives. Maybe long-term placement for your loved one or bring in reinforcements. You should not feel guilty about placing a loved one in the hands of a competent facility. Everyone's situation is different; some do not have the skills, ability, patience or time to care for their loved one at home.

Love does not dishonor. When a person is sick, their emotions can be raw. The ill person is already dealing with feelings of not being able to do what they are accustomed to doing. It is important that the caregiver cares for the person in a way that make them feel honored. We do not want our loved ones to feel like we do not want to care for them. How we care for them will let them know if we are doing it in love or out of obligation.

The whole concept of love and obligation can be confusing for the caregiver as both can be displayed at any given moment. Obligation has to do with doing out of a sense of duty which is not necessarily a bad thing. I believe the marital vows instill in us a sense of obligation or responsibility to the ones we commit to for the rest of our lives. But remember, acting simply out of obligation will not bring the joy that we desire in life. Those who do out of obligation alone will soon realize that no one can force them to do anything that they do not want to do. Caring for a loved one out of obligation will cause the caregiver to become burnt out physically, spiritually and emotionally. Doing out of duty may also bring tremendous guilt.

During my years as a caregiver, I have acted out of obligation. In those times when I felt as if what I was offering was being rejected and I wanted to walk away from my life, it was the sense of obligation, responsibility, and commitment that cause me to keep trying. Obligation is what gets me out of the bed some days, but love is what keeps me caring day after day.

Love is not self-seeking. Love allows me to care for my husband's needs even when I feel that my needs are not being met in return. Kindness is displayed because of the love that I have for him. There are times I have to use tough love, and he does not receive it as love but I try to accompany it with a heart of kindness.

There are days when I serve strictly out of obligation. This is not good, but in that moment it is the best I feel I have to offer. My daily prayer is that God will help me to demonstrate His love as I care for my husband. In those moments when I feel more annoyance than love, it helps to remember that if I can show the love of Christ I have succeeded. It is because of Christ that I can do what I am unable to do on my own.

To love as Christ loves means putting aside your own agenda to care for another. God loved us so much that He gave His only Son. His Son loved us so much that He laid down His life for us. We must love one another in such a way that Christ can be revealed in all that we do.

There is no glory or fame in being a caregiver. You may get minimal acknowledgements from others. You may or may not get acknowledged by the one you care for. Remember, love is not self-seeking; love does for others before she does for herself. Some caregivers never receive a thank you from the person they care for. Many people who are ill fail to acknowledge those who care for them.

Thankfully, my husband verbally expresses his appreciation to me. He is frequently saying "thank you." While I do believe he is appreciative, at times I wish his appreciation would translate into being more compliant.

If you are a caregiver who seldom hears the words thank you, know that what you are doing is valuable and I send a thank you to you today. The Lord knows the good you are doing and will not forget.

Love is not easily angered. When your ill family member yells at you, love does not get angry. When you make a nice meal, and he does not want it after he asked you to cook it, remember to show love. There will be many chances to feel rejection and heartache when caring for a loved one, but love does not keep a record of wrongs.

Love does not delight in evil but celebrates with the truth. It always protects. This could mean that you protect someone's spirits. You defend their integrity. You shelter their emotions.

Protecting my husband's spirits has been a focal point in my role as caregiver. I have to listen to what has not been said and know when it's time to call in friends or family to lift my husband up emotionally.

My husband will sometimes battle against what I am trying to do, but I am only thinking of what is best for him. I must remind myself that he an adult and although I am his caregiver, he still wants to make his own decisions. There are times that I have to remind him that he can trust me to do what is best for him. It is not my desire to harm him but to help him. His pain medication is very expensive, there are times when he does not want me to purchase it. Even though I understand his hesitancy to spend such a large amount of money, such a request is inhumane and I must put aside his wishes. As his wife, he wants me to respect and honor his request but as his caregiver I know he needs his medication. Therefore, it is my responsibility to make the necessary adjustments to obtain his medication.

Loving can be a huge assignment. My communication with my husband has been broken by his illness. He is more defensive about issues and is easily intimidated and irritated. Dealing with this in love and kindness is not always easy for me.

Chronic illness does great damage to the self-esteem of a person. When one feels unable to contribute in what they consider a meaningful way, their self-esteem is harmed. What I try to stress to my husband is that what is significant to him may not be important to me. A simple thing like eating at mealtime is huge for me. But often he will say no at mealtime only to ask for something later after I have moved on to another task. I try not to let it show, but sometimes he can sense my frustration.

Everything I do as a believer must reveal love. It can be difficult to practice love when you are met with resistance multiple times a day. When I become rude, impatient, and frustrated, I must go back to what the Scripture teaches about love and ask myself how I would want to be treated.

God commands that we love one another even when we do not love what the person does or how the person treats us. We must understand that loving is different from accepting or condoning negative behavior. We can love a person but not agree with the things they do or the way they behave.

The differences that couples experience in marriage can usually be worked out. But when a spouse becomes ill and the other spouse is the caregiver, the bulk of the responsibility has been placed on the caregiver. The caregiving spouse must love their spouses and care for them in a way that pleases God. Even when the spouse is in pain and lashing out, the caregiver must act in love.

My experiences in caring for my husband are unique to our situation. I do not believe there is one cookie-cutter plan that will work for every spouse/caregiver relationship. Each day is unpredictable, ever changing, and unique. But regardless of the situation, I as the caregiver must be ready to adjust accordingly. I always remember to ask God to help me show love and kindness as I care for Scott.

The caregiver wife shows love by caring for her husband's needs in a loving way. Her tone is one of love and compassion even when there are challenges in the relationship. Frustration can cause one to raise their voice and want to retreat. This is perfectly normal behavior for a married couple but it becomes more complex when caring for an ill spouse.

It is my natural instinct to prevent a problem before it arises. My husband's condition manifests itself in cycles. There are periods when he is in the wheelchair. Sometimes he uses a four-leg walker and other times he is able to ambulate with a cane. With his cyclic illness in mind, we try to restrict his activity as not to exacerbate his condition. Therefore, if I see him standing for a period, I will remind him that he should sit down. He usually responds, "I am fine, and I do not want to sit right now." Needless to say, he continues to stand on his feet for as long as he wishes or is able. Whichever comes first. The next day he will complain that his legs are painful and weak. In my mind this could have been avoided if he had followed my advice the day before. I have to now listen to the complaints and on some occasions, I have had to drive him to the doctors as a result of him overexerting himself. There have been times that his over activity has led to a hospital admission followed by inpatient rehabilitation for several weeks.

Honestly, on such occurrences I do not feel like responding in love. His actions have made my life as a caregiver more difficult. I do not have any strong words of wisdom to share regarding this matter as I still struggle with dealing with his disobedience and how it touches my life. It requires effort to present the characteristics that Apostle Paul writes about. It is a daily walk. When I look at the added stress his disregard for wise counsel has added to my life, I must purpose to walk in love.

His hospital admission as a result of overexertion may have added daily visitations to my schedule. To walk in love, I have learned to see the positive side of his being hospitalized. This time can be used as a time of respite for me. I also look at the fact that he was able to do something he wanted to do even though it did not end the way he wanted it to. In such a situation as this, I am learning to be less frustrated. See the brighter side of the situation and allow God to take care of the rest.

My chore is to love even when I do not agree. If I am to be an example of love, I must commit myself daily to love my husband in a way that is pleasing to God. This requires prayer and God's grace upon my life—Him doing for me what I cannot do for myself. Grace is God acting generously in our lives to do what we cannot do on our own. God's grace is readily available to me even when I did not deserve it.

After all, that is how the grace of God works. None of us deserve it, but He gives it freely to all who will receive it. His grace is readily available to all who call upon His name and as a caregiver; we have to call upon His name often. We will not be able to show the God kind of love without the help of God. When we call upon Him, He will hear our cry.

I would like to be able to offer some profound insight as to how I met and conquered the challenge to show love and to be kind, but I am still trying. One thing I have discovered on my journey is that the relationship between the two people prior to the illness has a huge impact on the relationship during the caregiving experience. Many of the problems that we are experiencing during my husband's illness were present before I became his caregiver.

In the early years of our marriage, we were focused on raising our children and building a ministry. In addition to that, my husband worked a secular full-time job that required some traveling. This left little time to focus on building a strong bond between the two of us. So when life became less busy, it forced us to look at what our foundation was built on. We had spent very little one-on-one time together, and now we are in a place where we are together every day. I imagine it is similar to what some couples feel after retirement, but add to that a major illness.

Some of the annoying things that we overlooked along the way now had to be confronted. This was difficult because at this point in our lives it was not about strengthening the marriage, but it was about survival. We were facing one crisis after another. We were always in crises-fighting mode. We were constantly putting out one fire only to have another one blaze up. I sometimes look at my husband and do not recognize the person he has become as a result of this illness. I wonder if he says the same about me.

If both people in the relationship are strong-willed and confrontational before the illness, this problem would now need to be addressed. There is no running out the door to work or children to cause distractions.

Many of the snags that develop in relationships can be masked in the busyness of life. But when life is no longer demanding, the issues will require attention.

On the other hand, if both the caregiver and the patient are mild-mannered, quick to compromise, or just neutral and laid back, I believe this carries into the caregiving journey. When both have calm personalities, this can make for a peaceful, tranquil environment.

Scott and I married at the age of thirty-one, and both of us had lived alone and established careers by that time. We each had our own way of doing things, and because life had been so busy for us it was never a real issue. Certainly, we had challenges along the way, but because of other things happening in life, we advanced forward. We hoped to someday figure things out but never really took the time or put in the necessary work.

Then I became the designated caregiver for him. His illness would change him into someone that at times I did not recognize, and I searched for bits and pieces of the man I knew or at least who I had perceived him to be. Now and then when we were around other people, he would make a special effort and I could catch a glimpse of the happy, carefree man I had married. But when we were alone, his demeanor would often change.

I understood what he was doing; he was trying hard to not let others see the pain he was experiencing. When he was home, he could relax. I had become his safe place to complain. I would hear people say, "He never complains." And he did not complain in their presence. But they were only around him for a few moments at a time.

To protect his image, my predicament was how do I ask for help and let others know my struggle as a caregiver when they think I have the ideal patient? And the greater question was, "Will our marriage be strong enough to survive this upset called sickness?"

The vows we said for better or worse, in sickness and in health would now be tested. Would I be able to stand by my words? Would I be able to show kindness to him even in the middle of conflict? In the hustle and bustle of life you never think you will come to this place in life. Sure he was hyper, and I was calm but some would say that we balanced each other out. But in his illness when he went through his angry phase, my calm demeanor only served to agitate him more. He wanted me to show strong emotions like he did, but that is just not who I am. I tend to keep my emotions inside which is not good but that is just who I am. I prayed that our children would not be adversely affected by what they were living with.

For example, as I mentioned earlier Scott would call me from the hospital regarding his frustration with the care he was receiving. In some cases, it was valid but I think most of it was just from spending so much time in the hospital. He felt as if control had been taken away from him and there was nothing he could do about it. So he would grasp control wherever he could get it. He would leave the service of a physician because he did not like what they said or disagreed with their treatment. While normally a valid reason, but when you have a chronic illness that there is no cure for, you cannot leave a physician because he does not cure you.

The frustration that he normally took out on me was now directed at those who cared for him in the inpatient setting. He was unhappy with the food in the cafeteria, did not like the way housekeeping cleaned his room, or the rooms were too hot or too cold. He could not be satisfied.

There were relationship issues that surfaced during his illness. I responded with frustration and distancing myself from him emotionally. Sickness does not bring out the worst in all people but for us this is what happened. All of the negativity, frustrations, shortcomings, and failures were all magnified. My solution was to go into self-survival mode. I could still be his caregiver but would not allow myself to be pulled into the emotional turmoil. We both became emotionally bankrupt and had nothing to offer each other.

Prior to his illness, as parents, we were happy with our children and for the most part content with our life as it was, but his illness changed everything. It became progressively difficult to reason with him regarding medical issues and personal issues. Some of it may have been related to all the medication that he had been given over the years, and his cognitive intellectual abilities were compromised. Things that he normally did quickly took extra time to process. He was forgetful but functional.

His unwillingness to follow doctors' orders became another source of frustration for me. The instructions that were given in an effort to assist him were often met with great resistance. What I had to resolve as his caregiver was that I could not force him to do what he did not want to do, and I had to be okay with his decisions. I had to learn to be kind to myself. Not stressing over what I could not change was a form of showing kindness to myself. I had to remind myself that my health was also important. I considered taking care of myself–showing kindness to myself. His neglect of following instruction was not being kind to himself. As a result, I would have to let it go and whatever the outcome we would deal with it at that time. That was the kindest thing that I could do for both of us. My badgering only served to aggravate him more.

My husband was always and continues to be extremely giving; doing what he thought pleased me without listening when I would tell him what I needed. I had shared with him many times that my love language was acts of service, not gifts, but his love language was gifts, so he kept bringing me gifts. Eventually, I stopped trying to explain to him and accepted that gift giving was what he was good at. He took great fulfillment in being able to give and provide financially for his family. That was an area he was highly confident in, and he did it well. He showed kindness by giving.

When his illness left him unable to work, he was at a loss not knowing what to do. I think this is fairly common among men. He felt that he had let the family down. I would explain over and over that because of some of the choices he had made things would be taken care of. No matter how many times you tell people how noble they are, they must believe it themselves. At times, I felt like I was pouring into an empty tank with holes in it.

Great effort will be needed to show kindness, and gentleness when caring for a loved one. I have heard it said of those who care for people who suffer from Alzheimer's or dementia that even though they may not know who you are, the person can sense if you are kind. People know when you love them by the attitude in which you care for them.

Kindness is transmitted in our actions, not words. It is more about how you do something and less about what you do. My mental structure is one of a doer. This has proven to be a blessing to me as a former nurse in that I could perform my duties without developing a deep emotional attachment to my patients. Learning to be kind to strangers and expecting nothing in return allowed me to set healthy boundaries. Sure, I have stories of patients that touched me in a deep way, but it is important that healthcare workers find balance.

In caring for my husband, it was difficult for me to transition from wife to caregiver and back to wife. My role as a caregiver put me in the mode of solving the problem, but what he needed most was for me to display kindness.

My personality is one that if you oppose me and are rude to me, I can still function in taking care of your needs. That is a problem when you care for a loved one because the functionality of the chore does not always show kindness. Even if the caregiver is not rude in return, the person can sense that it has become a task and not an act of kindness.

My temperament is one that has a strong desire for things to be perfect. This is an unrealistic expectation but nevertheless I continue to be bothered by the small defects in life. Another element of my temperament is that I can become consumed with doing and neglect the kindness factor. These are areas that I am constantly working to improve.

Kindness is something that I strive to show to my husband as his caregiver. It is important that he knows he is loved even when he can no longer perform his daily task. Showing kindness in the menial task of life can be most meaningful. It is found in the way I speak to him, the way I respond to the same question I answered five minutes ago. Tone is everything, and this is an area on which I continue to strive to do better in.

My husband will ask me a question and I will answer. He will ask the same question the third or fourth time and when I respond, it is a challenge not to grow impatient especially when he insists that he has not asked the question before. I sometimes think it would be easier if he admitted that he has memory issues. But then that is part of the memory issue process, a person not recalling that they did not remember something before, and if they do not recall that they didn't remember, then they will never admit to having a memory problem.

During the difficult phase of life as a caregiver, God will place people in your life to show you kindness. While growing up, I would hear my mother say, "God will not put any more on you than you can bear." It was during some of the darkest days as a caregiver I would think, "I cannot bear this." It was in those moments I understood what my mother was saying. It is in the darkest moments that God provided people to assist me in carrying the load. The assistance of others makes the load bearable. Learning to not only show kindness but be open to receive kindness from others gave me great encouragement as a caregiver.

Treating others the same way you want to be treated is a foundational truth from God's Word. If we can do this, we will be people who exhibit kindness on a daily basis. Whether it be caring for a loved one or relating to the grocery clerk, let's strive to be kind.

Prior to his illness, my husband was one of the kindest people I know. He was kind to friends, family and strangers alike. His illness has altered his overall personality, but he has managed to retain many of the traits of kindness. From experience, I know that the caregiver usually receives the worst of the illness. I am usually the one who gets the harsh criticisms even though I am the one who does the most for him. He often apologies for his critical attitude, but within the next few moments he will often repeat the action he just apologized for. I can sense his frustration of not being able to fully function while not liking the way he treats me.

When I first became my husband's caregiver, my feelings would get hurt multiple times a day. Finally, I came to understand that the way I felt about what he said or did was my responsibility. I realized that I had control over how I felt and more importantly, how I responded. His words may have been hurtful, but that did not mean that I had to take his words for truth. He was hurting, frustrated, and tired of the limitations that his illness had put on him. In an effort to relieve his frustration, he would project his negative feeling to me. As a result of many prayers uttered for me, I got to the point where it was no longer necessary for me to defend, qualify, or explain myself. My objective was to show kindness to the man I had pledged to love and leave the rest in the hands of God.

As caregivers, we must remember to be kind to ourselves. Illness is not a reason to allow others to treat us unkindly, and it is not a license for us to be unkind to the ones we care for.

Pray asking God to help you to show kindness and to love with the love of Christ.

Use your accompanying journal to write what you are feeling after you have prayed.

Lonely Heart

"What, then, shall we say in response to these things? If God is for us, who can be against us? He who did not spare his own Son, but gave him up for us all—how will he not also, along with him, graciously give us all things? Who will bring any charge against those whom God has chosen? It is God who justifies. Who then is the one who condemns? No one. Christ Jesus who died—more than that, who was raised to life—is at the right hand of God and is also interceding for us. Who shall separate us from the love of Christ? Shall trouble or hardship or persecution or famine or nakedness or danger or sword? As it is written: "For your sake we face death all day long; we are considered as sheep to be slaughtered." No, in all these things we are more than conquerors through him who loved us. For I am convinced that neither death nor life, neither angels nor demons, neither the present nor the future, nor any powers, neither height nor depth, nor anything else in all creation, will be able to separate us from the love of God that is in Christ Jesus our Lord" (Romans 8:31-39).

A few years ago, I was asked by my husband's physician if I would sit with some reporters to speak about the impact illness has on the caregiver. The hospital was conducting a caregiver's conference, and as advertisement for the conference, they wanted to hear from a real caregiver. I agreed to speak with the reporters without hesitation because I clearly understood how my life had been impacted. I met with three different reporters, two from local papers and one from radio. I was happy to share with them the impact my husband's illness had on our family. The loneliness and isolation of it all was and continues to be one of the most difficult parts of being a caregiver.

The caregiver is so often overlooked. The caregiver wants to be seen, heard, and understood. The caregiver does not want to just be the person pushing the wheelchair. The caregiver is a real person with real emotions and real pain. Their pain may not be physical, but it is nonetheless painful. The physical component of the illness may be limited to one person, but the psychological implication impacts the entire family. The caregiver is on the front line receiving the majority of the frustration the patient experiences.

The loneliness factor becomes very significant when caring for a spouse. When the dream of *happily ever after* is gone, what do you do? The long walks on the beach and gazing out over the ocean are memories of the past. You had a partner, someone you thought would always be there. You loved the person you married, but what about the person your loved one is today? You loved your healthy husband, but do you love your unhealthy husband? You love his strength, but what about his weakened state? You loved his take charge and handle it attitude, but now you are in charge and handling everything.

When I first got married and people would ask me what is the best thing about being married. For me it was the confidence of knowing that I had someone in my corner. No matter what happened at work or in life someone was on my side.

I may have had the worst day at work or the most exhausting day at home, but I was assured that my husband would always support me one hundred percent even if I was wrong. I would never have to face trouble, problems, or disappointment alone. Loneliness was not in my future as long as I was married to Scott Taylor.

Lonely Heart

Loneliness is a feeling of emptiness on the inside. You may feel isolated or disconnected from everything. The life of a caregiver is a lonely life. The type of loneliness you feel as a caregiver relates to missing what you have become accustomed to. The caregiver feels alone and out of contact with people because her life is consumed by her caregiving duties.

The caregiver's isolation can also be emotional isolation. There may be people all around you, but you have difficulty reaching out to them. You are emotionally disconnected from them and loneliness manifests. Many times, the caregiver is unable to express the feelings of their heart. People will ask, "Do you need to talk?" But it can be difficult to articulate your feelings. Finding the right words can be difficult especially when you are not sure of what you are feeling. Often the caregivers themselves do not even understand the assorted emotions felt, therefore it becomes impossible to share their emotions with others.

Loneliness is a huge problem when caring for your spouse. This is the person you committed to share your life, developed an intimate bond with, and you have history and memories, good and bad, with this person. But when this person is ill and suffering, every ounce of their energy is focused on them trying to make it through the next moment. They have little left to offer anyone else.

My husband complains about so many things on a daily basis. His health, his doctors, the way he looks, the pool man not doing a good job, the lawn not being cut right and on and on. His illness has affected him in such a profound way and as a result, nothing is done well enough for him. He went through a period in his illness when he isolated himself in his own little world and everything was about him.

If the doctors could not take his phone call in the middle of the day that meant they were too busy to take care of him. Never mind that the doctors had hundreds of patients. He felt as if he was the only one. One of my friends told me I spoiled him too much by catering to him. I am sure he would not agree with that statement, but it is evident when he goes in the hospital and he has the unrealistic demands from hospital staff. His behavior is one of "I am the only patient." His normal personality is one that holds others to a high standard. In his illness, this translated into nearly impossible to please.

Caregiving at any level is difficult. Although each situation is different, they are also similar. I speak as a wife taking care of her husband; this situation has its own unique set of challenges. For the chronically ill husband, all of his energy is focused on coping with the illness. So much so that it is extremely difficult or perhaps impossible to emotionally support the wife.

My husband would try to show concern if I verbalized a complaint, but it is usually short-lived. His pain most of the time is so high that when he tried to focus on what I may need, the pain he is experiencing will almost always inevitably revert his attention back to his condition. For me as the wife this is isolating. Although I am a caregiver, I still need someone to show concern for what I am feeling or maybe needing. My emotions are not turned off just because I am caring for him.

Throughout the past years there have been days when I was not feeling good. It would have been nice to have someone look after me. He tried to take care of me one year when I had the flu but I was busy trying to keep away from him. I did not want him to be infected with the flu virus. It was comical to witness the sick, taking care of the sick.

There have been other times when I have mentioned a problem that I was facing with my own health and he has never remembered to asked me about the outcome.

You enter the marriage thinking the two of you will have a wonderful life. Illness changes all of that, including responsibilities. There are many things the ill spouse can no longer be a part of both physically and emotionally. There is a great sense of loss that is experienced and the caregiver can become very lonely.

I have spent many hours feeling isolated and alone. Feeling as if no one sees me or what I need. Even though my husband is ill, my hopes and dreams for life are still very much a part of who I am. The plans we had made as a couple for our empty nest years and what was I expected to do with the rest of my life remained a great desire of mine. Nothing really had changed except for one thing, my husband was ill. I had to keep moving forward, living with what life had given me.

I share this because I want to encourage others who may be in the same place. The life you now have is certainly not the one you would have chosen for yourself, but it is the one you have. Loneliness is different from just being alone. Loneliness is the sense of being alone and feeling sad about it. We all enjoy being alone from time to time, but when we are lonely because we have no options available to us, then it becomes an actual problem.

Without a support system, caregivers often become isolated, which can lead to depression and other serious health issues. The good news is that there are ways to cope with feeling alone.

What I found helpful in dealing with my loneliness was to identify the feeling and expressing it. Journaling and even writing this book has been life altering for me. Counseling is also helpful. Many caregivers will not have the luxury of becoming involved in outside activities. Your time will not allow you to take on any other chores, but sometimes just phoning a friend can help to curb the feelings of isolation and loneliness.

It is so important that the caregiver be surrounded with friends and family. People who do not expect anything from you and do not expect you to behave in any particular way. If you want to talk it is okay, and if you do not want to talk, that is okay too. These are the people you want in your circle.

What I have found to be true in most cases and certainly in my situation is that with an extended illness the visits from others become less and less over time. When your loved one is first diagnosed, everyone wants to visit, but with each hospitalization the visits grow fewer. Being in the hospital has become the norm, and people do not respond as they did when he was first diagnosed. People have busy lives and I understand completely, but understanding does not make the caregiver less lonely.

My husband and I both enjoyed it very much when friends would come to visit our home, but because of my husband's condition we have limited our interaction with others. He is constantly in pain which makes it difficult for him to schedule time with visitors. It is uncomfortable for him to sit for an extended period. Also, when people would come my husband would try to entertain them which led to physical exhaustion for him.

When friends and family want to visit from out of town, we direct them to the nearest hotel. Even though we have plenty of room, emotionally I cannot handle an overnight guest. It is not that you do not want visitors, but that visitors can sometimes create more work for the caregiver. The caregiver's hands are already filled with many tasks.

There were times when friends or family would visit and they would offer to assist with household chores, things my husband could no longer do. Change high ceiling light bulbs, put salt in the water filtering tank and such. My husband would refuse help and get upset with me if I would accept. I was hesitant to reach out for help when I felt overwhelmed because I did not want to distress him. I did not really understand that; I would have thought he would jump at the chance for his wife to have some relief. But in his mind, it was highlighting another thing he was no longer able to do.

During the early years of his illness, I did it myself to keep from upsetting him. Eventually, the stress both physically and emotionally of caring for a loved one will take its toll on the body. I no longer desire to climb a ladder or lift heavy salt bags. Heights made me dizzy, and I did not want to fall off the ladder. My energy is not what it was, I fatigue quicker, and I have noticed that I get sick more often. Also, when I do get sick, the sickness last longer now due to the stress my body is under. Part of it could be age related, but I am careful to not dismiss the component that stress plays into it as well.

When you are stressed, your body produces the hormone cortisol. Cortisol helps the body manage stress but in high levels it interferes with the immune system exposing the body to disease.

I am learning to manage my stress, trying hard to do all within my power not to end up damaging my own health. After all, if I became ill who would care for my husband?

As a caregiver, when people offered, I started saying yes and sometimes I would ask them even if they did not offer. Just because my husband was isolating himself did not mean I had to isolate myself as well. Asking for help would mean a confrontation later with my husband, but I was prepared to deal with that if it meant getting a chore taken care of and relieving some of my stress. I also knew that our friends and family did not mind helping, they did not consider it a burden but a pleasure. In most cases, they were more than willing as they wanted to show their love in some way. Allowing them to assist in a chore was an opportunity for them to reach out to us and show kindness.

Friends and family have helped us by sitting with my husband at home and in the hospital, doing odd jobs around the house and even cooking dinner so I would not have to. Some have offered to help with cleaning our home for us. These people are a godsend to me. They truly make me feel blessed.

As caregivers, we must give others the opportunity to assist us in whatever way they can. Caregivers who are under great stress can develop diseases and premature death. While it is true that stress in the life of a caregiver cannot be avoided, it can be managed. This is not easily accomplished, but it is possible.

While it is nice to surround yourself with friends, seeing other couples doing things and having fun can sometime serve as a reminder to the caregiving spouse what is missing in their life. The emptiness in one's own relationship can cause the caregiving spouse to withdraw and pull away from married friends.

The laugher is a reminder of what you have lost. While I did not begrudge anyone of their happiness, especially my friends, being with them sometimes was a reminder of what was missing in my own life. Yes, there were times when I chose to isolate myself to avoid feeling the sting of discouragement. I had to learn what made me feel uncomfortable and what served as discouragement to me.

One Sunday morning while listening to a powerful sermon, I experienced a life-altering moment. The Scripture text was John 5:1-15 dealing with a man healed at the pool of Bethesda. The message spoke to me and to my current situation that Sunday morning. As the pastor, began to expound on the Word of God, I sat and listened, contemplating the changes that had taken place in our family as a result of my husband's illness. I made a decision that day that my days of having pity parties were over. I would no longer sit and wonder why or what if, but that I would adjust my attitude to accommodate my situation.

While I would like to tell you that I have never had a sad thought about my situation since, but that would not be true. There are days I give myself permission to take a moment to complain, but I choose not to linger there. I understand that if I remain too long in a mindset of disappointment and think about, "What if," it will cause me to become depressed. The "what if" thoughts do not benefit anyone because such thoughts do not change our situation.

Lonely Heart

I am my husband's caregiver, and that is who I am. My role as his wife is still binding, but he needs a caregiver more than he needs a wife at this time and I had to come to terms with that. At times, it is difficult for me to distinguish my roles, they are similar but in some ways very different.

In an effort to support and encourage me, people would remark on how difficult my job must be as a caregiver. I would respond, "What else would I do, I am his wife." But over time the demands kept coming and caregiving became a full-time job. Being the strong, independent woman I am, I should have been able to do it all, or so I thought. Now after doing this for nearly nine years, I know that not every wife does what I do. I am not judging or criticizing because this is a hard job and not everyone can do it. There are times that I wonder if I will be able to finish strong with no regrets.

There are spouses that walk away because they cannot handle the challenge. Some succumb under the pressure and divorce. Illness can lead to divorce thereby perpetuating the loneliness.

> *A total of 515 married patients were initially entered into this study with either a malignant primary brain tumor or MS. Two hundred fifty-four patients were female. Sixty marriages ended in either separation or divorce after the diagnosis of serious illness. This event was found to be significantly correlated with gender: 20.8% of relationships ended when the woman was the affected partner compared with only 2.9% when it was the man.*[1]

---

[1] Glantz, Michael J., Marc C. Chamberlain, Qin Liu, Chung-Cheng Hsieh, Keith R. Edwards, Alixis Van Horn, and Lawrence Recht. "Gender Disparity in the Rate of Partner Abandonment in Patients with Serious Medical Illness." *Cancer* 115.22 (2009): 5237-242. Web.

There are children who care for parents who physically abused them in childhood. Now as adults themselves they must care for the abusive parent. There are caregivers who care for spouses who have been abusive in the marriage. The role of caregiver can be marred and complicated to navigate.

Over time people seem to forget the sacrifices that caregivers make. You become known simply as the caregiver. That is just who you are and caregiving is what you do. The isolation for the caregiver is real whether the relationship with the one you care for was good or bad.

It has been a daily challenge for me to combat loneliness while living with an ill husband. Not wanting him to feel bad, I tend to keep my feelings inside. I don't want my husband to feel like he has failed me in any way. Many caregiver wives suffer in silence because of this belief. But in the process of their silence, there is One to whom they can take their troubles and distress. He will not tell anyone else about it and He will help us to carry the load. In many cases, He will carry the load for us. We have a friend in Jesus. We can take all our cares and concerns to Him in prayer.

God has provided exactly what we needed when we needed it. We have experienced some of the most enormous outpouring of love from friends and family. People have offered to ride with us to out of town doctors' appointments. People have volunteered to take my husband to appointments so I could be free to do other things. God has proven to be faithful in providing us with support to carry the heavy load we have.

Remember that nothing can remove you from the reach of a loving God. "Be strong and courageous. Do not be afraid or terrified because of them, for the LORD your God goes with you; he will never leave you nor forsake you" (Deuteronomy 31:6).

Lonely Heart

Pray asking God to build strong godly relationships in your life.
Use your accompanying journal to write what you are feeling after you have prayed.

See Me Hear Me Know Me

Heart of Patience

"Therefore, since we have been justified through faith, we have peace with God through our Lord Jesus Christ, through whom we have gained access by faith into this grace in which we now stand. And we boast in the hope of the glory of God. Not only so, but we also glory in our sufferings, because we know that suffering produces perseverance; perseverance, character; and character, hope. And hope does not put us to shame, because God's love has been poured out into our hearts through the Holy Spirit, who has been given to us" (Romans 5:1-5).

Patience is a godly trait, vigorously working and persevering toward an end that will honor God. It works while it waits. Psalm 37:7 reads, "Be still before the LORD and wait patiently for him; do not fret when people succeed in their ways, when they carry out their wicked schemes." We are not asked to sit and do nothing attempting to demonstrate patience. We are however asked to depend totally on God, not to fret and this will demonstrate patience.

Patience speaks of bearing a misfortune without complaining. When faced with adversity, we have no choice but to bear it. The question becomes, how do we bear it? While we wait for deliverance from various situations in life, how do we wait? Do we wait complaining, fussing, and cussing while having a pity party for one? How we wait can dramatically affect our witness to others. Are people encouraged or discouraged by what they see when they look at us?

I was instructed early in life never to pray for patience because patience comes as a result of life challenges. The consequences of hard times are to cultivate patience in us and make us stronger and wiser. Patience has less to do with enduring a hard challenge, and more to do with how one endures. Complaining and getting angry or irritated is not a true representation of patience.

Living life will produce fortitude within each individual. It is the experience of going through the test that builds one's patience. The inability to tolerate whatever comes in life will not produce forbearance. Believers are encouraged to maintain an attitude of patience while enduring trials. Even in the midst of trying desperately to alter the situation, patience is important.

Some Bible translators have chosen the expression *longsuffering* as the most representative precise word for patience. The person who is longsuffering is one who suffers a long time and does not complain. Long could be days, months, or years depending on the situation. When you are waiting for medical reports, days can seem like months. While the amount of time can vary, the idea of whether we complain or not is the deciding factor of whether or not patience is revealed.

While we are travailing, are we thankful for the blessing in our life or are we irritable about everything? There are things that transpire in life that cause people to wonder why. There are times when a period of re-evaluation may be necessary. People make mistakes and in the process valuable lessons are learned. Once the error has been identified, a plan is put in place to avoid having to experience the same anguish again as a result of the same blunder.

If I pay close attention, I can learn from the mistakes of others. I do not believe you have to experience everything in order to learn. Even in my caregiver role, I have learned of some things that could have been done differently: perhaps better health choices or early medical attention.

I do not know or will never know if these adjustments would have altered our circumstance.

Looking back will not change your current situation, but it will give some insight for the future. Is the life of a caregiver considered suffering? If you dwell on the regrets of what you could possibly have changed, it can cause chaos.

During my caregiving experience, some days feel like a chastisement and I think, I did not sign up for all of this. Then I think if God picked me to care for one of His children, He knew I could handle such an important assignment. And I knew He would grace me to do whatever was necessary. This entire experience is building patience within me.

The enemy would have us live in fear and guilt of what we might have done, missed, or how we may have felt about our role as caregiver. But we must keep our eyes on the prize. Even if we experience trials and testing for a long time, God has not changed His mind concerning the plan He has for us. Not everyone gets the opportunity to care for the people they love. The role of a caregiver can be rewarding and inspiring.

A caregiver's job is not something that one plans and looks forward to doing. While it is an honor to be able to serve a family member in that capacity, it is one of life's challenges that many find themselves navigating through each day. Some days are better than others as it relates to patience. Caring for another adult with opinions and strong desires can be strenuous. How do you tell another adult that you know what is best for them? Especially when you are not sure, but the responsibility has become yours since you are the caregiver. When it comes to important medical decisions, it can be hard to make the decisions for yourself and now for another person. The undertaking can be overwhelming. Remember, you are part of a caregiving team. You do not need to make medical decisions without the assistance of your health care provider. Learn to use the access you have been given by those around you. If the patient is able, they may also want to have input. It is important to the patient that their opinion is not dismissed.

We communicate with my husband's primary physician by email most of the time. Periodically, a phone call might be necessary in between visits. Allowing others to assist you will keep you from getting so frustrated that you fail in the battle to win patience.

Some acts of impatience have awful consequences. Other acts of impatience produce mildly negative outcomes. Relationships can be affected when one or both parties neglects to exercise patience.

I have been guilty of impatience in the decision-making process. My husband will ask my opinion regarding a matter concerning his care. I will offer my opinion as his caregiver and he will disagree. In the midst of the conflict, I will say, "It's up to you." Most of the time we end up right back where we started doing what I suggested. If I had been more patient in relaying my opinion, the frustration could have possibly been omitted.

Patience is a virtue. We never know how much patience we will need until we are faced with a trying situation. It is easy to be on the outside looking in thinking you know what to do. But when you are faced with the situation, it is not as simple as it seems.

Because my husband struggles with memory issues, I frequently have to repeat things multiple times to him. He will often tell me that I did not tell him something that I know I shared with him before. This can be trying and I am constantly reminding myself, just tell him again. Sometimes my expression and voice tone will show my frustration.

Without patience, the voyage of being a caregiver will be nearly impossible, but patience increases with each new encounter. The Epistle of James reads in the first chapter and third verse that the testing of our faith produces patience. The goal of the testing or trials that we experience is not to destroy us but to build us.

My husband has a "do not resuscitate" order in his medical record. In my old nursing days, DNR meant if you stop breathing you were not to be resuscitated. Now, depending on which hospital you are in, there are specific treatments that the patient has to designate to be withheld. My husband has decided that he does not want chest compression, a breathing tube or to be fed through a tube. He also did not want a pacemaker to regulate his heart or blood products should they be needed.

On his recent admission his blood counts were very low, and he needed blood transfusions. When he called me on the phone, he said, "You told me not to have blood transfusions." That was not true, in fact the night before I left the hospital, I had stressed to him that he might want to consider transfusions because in the past blood transfusions had helped him breathe and feel better. When I got to the hospital, I spoke to the physician who told me that as long as the patient was alert and oriented, they had to follow to what he said. In my presence the doctor asked him, "What year is it? Where are you? Who is president?" Of course, my husband's answers were correct.

It was difficult to explain to the doctor who was meeting him for the first time the dilemma I face daily. It is not that he was altered mentally it is that he is forgetful, and I felt unable to make life and death decisions concerning his health. I requested the nurse in my presence to review the DNR order, and my husband decided to agree to blood transfusions. It is not that I wanted him to have unnecessary life-longing procedures; I wanted to be sure he understood what he was signing.

On several occasions, I have been accused of saying or doing something that I did not do or say simply because his memory is not as strong as it once was, and getting others to understand our plight is difficult. Each day presents a new opportunity to display patience not only with my husband but with those who care for him.

Looking back, I often wonder how I made it this far. If someone had told me nearly nine years ago that I would still be standing, I am not sure I would have believed them. But each challenge has built my stamina, improved my reserve, and enhanced my desire to persevere. The challenges that we face in life produce staying power within us.

There are great lessons to be learned in the midst of the storm. In fact, some of my most valuable trainings have been accomplished at great cost. I often say, "I would never want to go back to my young adult years." But if I could be a young adult again and have the same wisdom, I currently relish in my fifties, it would not be a negative experience for me. Because one of the things I have acquired over the years is more patience. I have learned that hardship in one area does not necessarily mean it is a completely destructive experience.

Adversity can birth opportunities. Learn to see God in whatever you experience in life and recognize that He will give you the patience you need to endure. You can come out of the test better, stronger, and wiser.

When the urge to be short-tempered appears, take a deep breath and know that God chose you from the foundation of the world. Everything you have ever done in your life has prepared you for this moment. All the challenges, the trials and the tests, have matured you to the level that you can accomplish this task without complaining.

Our need for patience will continue as long as we live on this earth. We will continue to face challenges each day. Some of the challenges we face will be great while others will be small, but patience will be needed nonetheless. The caregiver will need great patience to complete the task at hand.

My patience is most often tested when it comes to meal preparation. Cooking is not one of my strong suits nor do I enjoy it. My husband's appetite has diminished greatly. He loves sweets and bread, and mealtime is an area where my patience is tested daily. My husband enjoyed cooking and was very good at it, but now the majority of meal preparation is my responsibility. I am a very simple cook ... nothing fancy, but my expectation is that he will eat what I prepare. Of course he has other plans, and it can be a struggle to get him to eat. Usually I will ask him what he would like. He seldom offers a suggestion. So I will proceed to prepare what I think he might want. My feelings are, *since I do not like to cook and I made the effort, you have to eat it*. His thoughts are *I do not want anything to eat right now*. I grew up in an environment where it was said, "When you get hungry you will eat." Well, this is not the case with a person who is sick. A person who is sick may go days without eating. And as the caregiver, it becomes part of my chore to see to it that he eats every day. I need a double dose of patience at mealtimes.

Patience is secured in hope. And our hope is grounded in the promises of God. Patience enables us to inherit God's promises. When we live in a state of expectancy knowing that God will deliver, we can remain patient.

It can be difficult to be patient with a difficult person, even if it is someone you are caring for. Reflect on the patience that God has extended toward you and pray asking for His help in extending the same grace of patience to others.

Use your accompanying journal to write what you are feeling after you have prayed.

See Me Hear Me Know Me

Peaceful Heart

"May the God of hope fill you with all joy and peace as you trust in him, so that you may overflow with hope by the power of the Holy Spirit" (Romans 15:13).

Jesus gave peace to the disciples as He was about to leave them. *Shalom*, meaning peace was a normal farewell among the Jews. In Jesus' farewell, He adds *my peace*. This is not a predictable desire but Jesus is granting His special peace that expels distress and sadness from the mind. The peace that our Lord gives cannot be comprehended by man (John 14:27).

As a caregiver, there are many days that the peace of God will be needed. In the middle of undiagnosed diseases, uncertain treatment, undetermined outcomes, and fast-talking physicians, it is only through the peace of God one can discover rest. Just as Jesus spoke to the storms at sea, He can speak to the storm in your life. If the winds obey His voice, surely He has the authority to speak to turmoil in our lives.

Illness brings stress and turmoil, leaving it difficult to find peace. With all the thoughts going through your mind, it is hard to find rest. With every setback comes its own fear and doubt. Sickness brings new mountains to climb and new challenges to overcome.

The uncertainty of finances is a major adjustment when illness strikes. Illness brings with it an increasing mountain of medical expenses with no cure in sight. If we are not careful worry can set in. The Scripture admonishes us not to worry but to trust God. When we worry, it shows our lack of trust in God:

> *Therefore I tell you, do not worry about your life, what you will eat or drink; or about your body, what you will wear. Is not life more than food and the body more than clothes? Look at the birds of the air; they do not sow or reap or store away in barns, and yet your heavenly Father feeds them. Are you not much more valuable than they? Can any one of you by worrying add a single hour to your life? "And why do you worry about clothes? See how the flowers of the field grow. They do not labor or spin. Yet I tell you that not even Solomon in all his splendor was dressed like one of these. If that is how God clothes the grass of the field, which is here today and tomorrow is thrown into the fire, will he not much more clothe you—you of little faith? So do not worry, saying, 'What shall we eat?' or 'What shall we drink?' or 'What shall we wear?' For the pagans run after all these things, and your heavenly Father knows that you need them. But seek first his kingdom and his righteousness, and all these things will be given to you as well. Therefore, do not worry about tomorrow, for tomorrow will worry about itself. Each day has enough trouble of its own (Matthew 6:25-34).*

One of the many issues that caused me to be anxious was the possibility we would lose my husband's life insurance policy. We both had large policies and had talked about what to do in the event of either of our deaths. I had a private policy which was relatively inexpensive that I purchased when I was much younger. My husband's company paid a large portion of the premium for his life insurance policy, and we were comfortable with his coverage. After he was no longer able to work, we were given the option to continue the policy as a private pay. We were able to maintain it for a few years, but eventually we had to drastically reduce the coverage amount because it was too expensive. As his age went up so did the insurance premiums.

I did not want to lose the policy as I knew with his diagnosis it would be nearly impossible to secure an alternate policy. This change was a source of stress for me; he had been the family provider for many years. What would happen to our family if he passed away? How would I make the mortgage payment? How would the girls go to college?

I had been away from full-time clinical nursing since our daughters were born, and we had lived on his income. Where would I find a job that would cover our current expenses? And now with the added medical expenses how would I make the amount of money that would be needed to continue our current lifestyle. All of these thoughts ran through my mind.

I had to find peace in this unstable situation. Coming to the conclusion and realizing that God had already provided for every need that we would ever have brought me comfort.

The peace of God is for you even in the midst of your caregiving days. You have no need to worry or be anxious. When the funds are low and the expenses are high, you can go back to the Word of God. If God provides for the birds why would He not provide for your needs?

It is because of the grace of God that our family is still whole and intact today. God has proven Himself to be just who He says He is and has done more than we could ever ask or think. Ephesians 3:20 reads, "Now to him who is able to do immeasurably more than all we ask or imagine, according to his power that is at work within us."

God's power is unlimited; it extends beyond our imagination. Do not let your peace be disturbed by the lack of finances. Philippians 4:19 reads, "And my God will meet all your needs according to the riches of his glory in Christ Jesus."

Medical expenses are a huge part of having an ill family member. But there may be resources available in your community that can assist you. Check with the hospital as sometimes they have programs for those who are experiencing financial hardship. Do not let the mountain of debt disturb your peace.

Set up a payment plan to pay off your debt; companies will work with you. Peace is something that you cannot put a monetary value on. Having peace is more valuable than riches. Peace will allow you to get a good night's rest. It is possible to experience peace when things seem to be crumbling around you. It is in the times of great trial that you receive great victories. The Lord makes Himself known in the troubles of life as our Sufficiency. The psalmist tells us, "The righteous person may have many troubles, but the LORD delivers him from them all;" Psalm 34:19. God is well able to bring you out of any situation you may find yourself in.

Learn to rest in Him. Having the peace of God is better than fame or riches. The word peace speaks of tranquility, harmony, calmness, and quietness. In the most difficult situations of life, God can grant peace. He can calm the mind and still the voices of doubt that we hear in our head. Identifying the things that disturb your peace is half the battle. Once you have identified them, try to shun them if you can. For the caregiver, escaping is probably not an option. If you cannot escape them, learn how to cope with them. Accept the fact that you do not control the outcome that illness has taken on your family. You cannot predict what will happen. Leave it in the hands of God.

Seeking a moment of peace by having someone come in to relieve you may be an option, but what do you do when your loved one refuses the care of others? Perhaps they are fearful of a different person seeing them as they really are or they are convinced that you are the only one in the whole world that can care for them the right way.

My husband never wanted anyone to come take care of him other than me. Even when he was in the hospital, he did not want me to leave. This was very hard for me as a wife and caregiver. I needed a break and did engage the assistance of others on rare instances.

When you do have someone else come in, how do you come to terms with the fact that when you return from your time away your work has doubled? Maybe your loved one will agree to have a paid health care professional come in, but your budget will not allow you to bring in paid staff? Yes, each situation is different, but every caregiver needs time to relax and refresh. Find a space where you can relax, maybe sitting by the pool or just looking out of a window. When you feel your peace being disturbed, you may have to go to your peaceful place. This is a place where you can commune with your Heavenly Father. Music is a good soother for the soul. Have a few songs that will calm your heart and your mind ready to listen to at a moment's notice.

Feelings of guilt can disturb our peace. When caring for a loved one, sometimes we feel like we are not doing a good job. The only purpose the guilt serves is to disrupt our peace. Realize that for most of us we will never do the job others expect us to do or even what we expect of ourselves. Doing our best and doing it in love is all that is required.

In order for the caregiver to be at peace, the caregiver must first take care of themselves. Your heart and mind have to be at peace in order to care effectively for a loved one. Remember the source of your peace. Your peace comes from your relationship with Jesus Christ. He gives you His peace. He can bring harmony in the dysfunctional relationships that sometimes exist between the patient and the caregiver. Seek God for direction in your role as a caregiver. When you seek Him, He will be there to lead you all the way.

Maintaining your peace may require closing your mouth at times. When caring for a loved one who has been ill a long time, the person can be easily agitated. The smallest thing the caregiver says further disturbs the patient. To keep the peace in the house and in your life you may need to remain silent at times as a caregiver. Some things are not worth debating and usually do not solve the problem anyway. I find that when the mind is made up about an issue, it is not easily changed.

Another source of frustration for me is when I sit with my husband for long periods and he does not say anything. The moment I walk out the room he calls my name. I do not understand why this happens, but it does. Sometimes I will turn around and come back and other times I will say, "I will be back shortly." I sometimes need that extra moment to ensure that my peace remains intact so that when I do come back, I can do it with a smile and not a frown.

God desires to give us His peace, but we must seek after it. We must let go of the desire to be right, and we cannot be afraid of change. When things do not go the way we want them to go, we can choose to remain in peace or to lash out. It is better to remain at a place of peace if possible.

Pray, asking God to grant peace in the midst of your chaos.
Use your accompanying journal to write what you are feeling after you have prayed.

Quiet My Heart

"When anxiety was great within me, your consolation brought me joy"
(Psalm 94:19).

Quietness means having a time of solitude and relaxation—a time that is free of stress where you can experience calmness in the storms of life. Caregivers experience little time of quietness and relaxation. Caregivers have to manage the lives of the ones they care for while managing their own lives. If there are minors in the home, then that becomes an added responsibility for the caregiver.

The needs of the children cannot be overlooked. Often the caregiver must give extra attention to the children to compensate for what they may be missing, especially if the one being cared for is the other parent. The desire to shield the children can be stressful. Not wanting the children to worry, both parents may put on brave faces. Children are very intuitive and often can pick up on things even before they are told.

When my husband was first diagnosed, one of my struggles was my attempt to maintain a sense of normalcy in our home. We tried to do the things we had always done, but it eventually became increasingly more difficult as his health continued to decline. I remember stopping at a mall a few days before Christmas to do some shopping on the way back home from the hospital. My husband had been admitted to a hospital nearly two hundred miles from our home the week of Christmas. I think he was discharged the day before Christmas Eve. Not wanting our children to feel the impact of their father's illness, there had to be gifts under the tree for Christmas. When a parent is ill and the other parent is the caregiver, it becomes easy for the children to become lost in the chaos. The goal is to try to keep life as routine as possible.

I am sure our children knew something was not right as they were frequently dropped off and picked up by friends and neighbors for school. I would get delayed in a long doctor's appointment and have to arrange transportation at the last minute. There were times when friends would be asked to spend the night and get them off to school in the morning as I was spending the night at the hospital. Our high schooler received a car a few years earlier than planned as I needed her to assist with transportation and errands. Life can get very busy when someone in the home is struggling with a debilitating condition.

The caregiver will need a time of quietness to focus and plan for the future. Quiet time is essential to endurance. Taking on the role of caregiver can be overwhelming. When you lose a loved one, the event of death is a one-time event. After the grieving process, you move on to whatever is next. When you are a caregiver, the process is ongoing. You live in the expectancy that it will get better but with the reality that it may not. There is seemly no end in sight as the person's condition changes from day to day. The caregiver will need a place to go just to be quiet so that the spirit can be refueled. Every caregiver needs time to relax and refresh. This becomes vital to the caregiver's ability to continue to function at their optimal level.

The job of a caregiver can be restricting to one's lifestyle. Feeling like you are in captivity because of the limitations you experience daily is not uncommon. Being able to move about without constraint is something the caregiver does not usually experience. As you are responsible for caring for someone, your schedule becomes their schedule.

The uncertainty of the day-to-day planning can be overpowering. You get up in the morning with one plan and things can change without warning. Or you lay down at night expecting to sleep eight hours and maybe end up sleeping just a few. My sleep has been disturbed on multiple occasions in the middle of the night. I have to arise and carry out my duties as if it were eight o'clock in the morning. Illness does not recognize schedules or clocks. Waking in the middle of the night to administer medication and assist with other personal care needs can become the norm.

It is similar to having infants and young children; you cannot run out of the house on a moment's notice. And you never know what time your baby will wake you up in the middle of the night. Having a good plan is paramount but so is being willing to be flexible. While freedom is limited, it is beneficial to the caregiver to plan free moments throughout the day. It is vital to schedule time for yourself, whether it is a walk, lunch with a friend, or a mid-day nap. You may only have a few minutes to steal away, but use them. Caregivers need time to re-energize in order to be the best caregiver possible to their loved ones.

As a caregiver, I can tell you that freedom is a luxury. The process to schedule time away can be exhausting. It's great when a friend calls and says "Let's do lunch." If I had to plan it myself, then I would skip it. Just the thought of planning something else even for me many times is draining. The caregiver will need the support of a good friend who can sense when a time out is needed. It can be difficult to move away from the situation but if you have a friend who will take you away, that is very helpful. Give a friend permission to hold you accountable in that area.

The caregiver must not neglect time with God. Sometimes we can get so wrapped up in what we are doing that we forget the source of our strength. Prayer and devotional meditation is necessary to continue each day of caregiving. Think of it as intravenous spiritual vitamins that build us up from the inside out.

Listen to the Bible if you cannot get the time to read. Listen while you are doing some of your chores. Have someone sit with your loved one so you can go to worship services with other believers. Being in fellowship with others can encourage you and strengthen you.

My husband did not like for me to ask friends or neighbors to sit with him. And the few he did agree to, most were not available on Sunday morning. Occasionally, I would pay a sitter to come in for four hours on Sunday. This would give me time to drive to church, attend services and drive back home.

Having great music as a part of your life is another important component. Listen to music, it stimulates the soul. Apostle Paul writes, "Speak to one another with psalms, hymns, and spiritual songs. Sing and make music in your heart to the Lord," Ephesians 5:19. Your passion for the things you love should not be totally neglected.

Exercising is also another refreshing thing that can benefit the mind and the body. I work out in the gym in the morning; this is a time for me to strengthen my mind and body. It also keeps me on track because it is so easy to sit on the couch and snack. Exercise is like therapy for me. If I was unable to exercise, it would be very disappointing.

Some evenings I spend time walking in my neighborhood. This is a time of quietness for me. It's that getaway for me where I am not responsible for anything except walking and breathing deeply. My mind clears and endorphins are released which helps to lift my mood.

Finding quiet moments where and when you can is necessary. A caregiver receives minimal time alone, but it is so essential that they find the time. It is in the quiet moments you may hear God's whisper.

One thing I have learned after the first few years of caregiving was that when my husband is in the hospital, I no longer spend the night there with him. When he was first diagnosed and admitted to the hospital, we both checked in. I would spend nights and days there. I had someone stay with the girls at night and they were in school all day. On a good day, I would usually come home around three to make dinner for them and leave heading back to the hospital once they went to bed at night. There were days that I did not come home at all.

Once I realized that this was going to be a long-term thing, I made the decision not to spend the night at the hospital. I would use his inpatient time as a respite for me. This was tough for me because my previous career as a registered nurse compelled me to feel like I was always needed at the hospital. I wanted to know what was going on and be there every time the doctors came by. As prepared as I thought I was, my nursing degree had not prepared me for the constant level of stress brought on by caring for my husband. I became consumed by the process and I knew I needed to step back and take some quiet time.

I would need to trust God that the staff would take good care of him. And if I needed to speak with the doctors, I could call them on the telephone. I also learned to ask others for help with the visitation while he was inpatient. This would allow me free time to take care of some personal needs and do something that I enjoyed. This much needed free time was helpful to my mental attitude.

Time is a precious commodity; we all have the same amount of it. How we use it will determine our productivity in life. For the caregiver, quiet time is precious.

It may be difficult but the caregiver needs to remain involved in things that they enjoy. You are still allowed to have a life of your own as a caregiver. There should be no guilt experienced in allowing God to give you these opportunities of refreshment. He knows your needs and wants to bless you so that you can bless the one you care for.

Taking care of a loved one takes up a great deal of time. Being around friends can help to reduce your stress. You may not be able to be as active as you once were, but take advantage of every opportunity to interact with friends. Fun activities can help reduce stress in the life of caregivers. Laugh as much as possible; spend time with happy people and doing things that make you smile. Even if you have to steal moments out of your day, spend them doing enjoyable things.

There is no way to completely remove the stress that comes with being a caregiver. It is an exhausting process that leaves you emotionally, mentally and physically exhausted. The caregiver's stress must be managed in order to prevent a personal health crises for the caregiver.

Caregivers need to take time to recharge their body and mind to avoid becoming depressed. Getting out of the house is necessary to your mental and physical well-being. We can only accomplish so much. We cannot do it all. Your patient will benefit most from a refreshed caregiver.

Learn to say yes when others offer to assist. Do not be shy about delegating responsibilities to others. Keep yourself healthy by eating and exercising. Your freedom may be limited, but it has not been taken away. Set limits, you may sometimes have to say no, even to the loved one you care for. But on those days when you are unable to leave the house, you can rest in the liberty you have in Christ, knowing that He is able to meet all of your needs.

Pray asking God to help you use wisdom with the free time you have.

Use your accompanying journal to write what you are feeling after you have prayed.

Thankful Heart

"Give thanks in all circumstances; for this is God's will for you in Christ Jesus" (1 Thessalonians 5:18).

No matter how hard I try, there are those days that I spend too much time dwelling on the negative aspect of my life. What we think about can influence our mood. It is important to guard against negative thinking. I can testify that on those negative thinking days that is exactly how the negative thoughts make me feel. Negative. God wants us to be completely thankful for the blessings He has given us in our lives. Dwelling on negativity will not produce thankfulness.

When a person focuses on the negatives of life, it can only lead to sadness. Time spent dwelling on negativity can be better spent. When the mind begins to recall negativity, it is imperative that the negative thoughts be combated with joyful thoughts. If not, the negative thoughts will rule. As a result of the negative thoughts ruling, a person can become physically weak and physical symptoms begin to manifest, headache, dizziness, stomach aches, etc.

As a caregiver, it is easy to get caught up in the cycle of dwelling on the negative things that happen in life. Negative thoughts must be combatted quickly or the thoughts will take over. Expressing thankfulness will cause us to focus on what we have instead of what we do not have.

When caring for a loved one, there are many things that we wish we could change. The desire to have the person well again is always there. Life may not be as we would want it to be, but we must find a way to be thankful. Our situations may be tough, but there is always someone else with an equal or greater struggle. No one goes through life without experiencing some form of pain. We may not have everything we desire, and things may not be the way we want them but we have much to be thankful for. Even as a caregiver, we can be thankful that we are able to care for another person. It could have been that someone was taking care of us.

An attitude of thankfulness changes our outlook on life. When we are thankful, we do not worry as much. With more thankfulness, we have less anxiety. Being thankful brightens your day and all of those around you. The ability to express gratitude is healthy for the body, mind, and soul.

Proverbs 17:22 reads, "A cheerful heart is good medicine." A cheerful heart is a happy or a merry heart. If you want to keep your heart happy, learn to practice being thankful. Learn to offer thankfulness in any settings of your life. We can give thanks in the midst of whatever we may be experiencing in life.

There is nothing like the feeling of joy. It's an emotion that cannot be explained by one word. Joy has to do with a feeling of great happiness. Joy is also the source or cause of great happiness. Joy can be found in something or someone. And we can also be the conduit that brings joy to someone else. Many times we receive joy from doing for someone else or receiving something from another person.

Where is the joy in being a caregiver? Joy and sorrow can exist together. The situation, while not joyful, we can have joy in.

It is possible to be joyful while experiencing some of the darkest moments of life. As we learn to focus more on the larger picture and less on the incident we can experience joy.

I think back to when I was giving birth to my children. Certainly the experience itself was not joyful, but I was joyful because of the hope and expectancy that my discomfort would produce a healthy child.

Caregiving can be a joyful experience. While one is not joyful that a loved one is ill and needs care, the greater purpose is the fact that the other person is able to provide the care. We experience joy when we are able to give to others—when we are able to assist others in what they cannot do for themselves. Everyone needs to be loved and be able to give love. As a caregiver, we are in the awesome position to give love. How great is that? Knowing that brings joy to the heart of the caregiver. When we live in the presence of God, we experience His joy. In His presence is fullness of joy.

Taking care of a loved one who is ill presents many opportunities to be negative. It is a daily choice that I make, to be thankful. At times it is difficult to express thanksgiving, not because I do not have any reason to be thankful but because of the overwhelming negativity. On those days that I cannot find any joy in what I am doing as a caregiver, I find it helpful to talk it out with a friend.

Putting your feelings into words can lessen the emotional load. Support groups may be helpful as well. Just knowing that others know and understand what you are going through can be so helpful.

I personally did not find the support groups helpful. When I went to a support group, I left feeling sad. After hearing what others were dealing with, it broke my heart. I found private counseling to be helpful for me. The ability to talk and have someone to just listen does wonders.

Many times no guidance is needed; all you need is an attentive ear. Finding a trusted person to listen is a valuable gift. You have needs and will want to reach out to others for ideas, advice and assistance, and that includes finding ways to take care of the caregiver—you.

It is normal to feel overwhelmed at times. Relationships are complicated. Add illness and you have triple complications. Do not let others make you feel like you are a bad person because you are experiencing negative emotions. When we present a happy face in public, others will not know what is going on behind closed doors. As a result, they will think everything is fine and when you start to experience negative emotions, they will not understand where those emotions are coming from. Being thankful does not mean that we do not have challenges. There is always something that we can find to be thankful for even in the midst of chronic illness of a loved one. You can brighten your day by finding things to be thankful for.

In hard times, it can appear that God is far away and we feel alone. Being thankful is more than just saying "Thank you" although that is a good place to start. A heart of gratitude reflects our trust in God. Knowing that even though He seems far, we believe He is near. Psalm 30:5 reads, "For his anger lasts only a moment, but his favor lasts a lifetime; weeping may stay for the night, but rejoicing comes in the morning." We can be thankful that God is bringing us through. The journey may be difficult but we are moving forward with each passing day.

I look back at some of the hard times our family has already walked through and it gives me confidence to know that we will continue to move forward. God is always with me and my family even when I do not feel like He is. There is always evidence of His presence; I just need to open my eyes, heart and mind to see it.

Being thankful does not mean that we live in denial or ignore what we are experiencing. To have a heart of thanksgiving means that we look beyond our current situation and see the greater plan that God has for our lives. We see all that we have to be thankful for. Even in the most difficult times if you listed your blessing and your complaints, I promise you the thankful column would exceed the complaint column.

Over the course of my husband's illness and my years as a caregiver, we have experienced many blessings. Our two daughters have excelled academically and professionally. They are compassionate young women who have incredible hearts for others. I believe God will use their experience of what our family has endured in a way that blesses others.

In spite of the financial challenges we have had due to loss of full-time income, we are thankful that our needs have been met. We have not lost anything in the process, sure we have had to scale back in our lifestyle but we still have the necessities of life intact.

In the most challenging season of his illness, we desired to remain thankful. In recalling our first follow-up appointment we had with hematology oncology, we went in to see if he was responding to the initial chemotherapy regimen. It was at this appointment that we received the news that the chemotherapy was not working and that my husband's cancer had progressed.

The physician informed us that he was being admitted to the hospital immediately for around the clock chemotherapy. We were so new to the whole process at that time that we did not fully understand the concept of what we were hearing. We had prayed and believed God for good news at this appointment, instead what we received was that the cancer had not responded favorably to the chemotherapy.

Even with this negative report, we were thankful that God would be with us throughout the entire process.

Once he was all checked into the hospital, I left to go home. As I was waiting for the car, a lady I did not know approached me. I told her that my husband had been admitted to the hospital. As I spoke to her tears filled my eyes. I do not remember exactly what my thoughts were, but I did know that whatever happened, God was capable of handling the situation and I had to surrender it to Him. I was thankful that God places people to encourage us when we need it. Even though I did not know her, and she did not know me, God knew us both.

Philippians 4:6 reads, "Do not be anxious about anything, but in every situation, by prayer and petition, with thanksgiving, present your requests to God." When we come before God with requests, the Bible teaches that we are to come with thanksgiving. When we accept that God is in control of everything and He knows why and when things will happen, we can be thankful. We begin to understand that complaining does not change anything. God responds to our thanksgiving, we may not get the answer we desire but we can be sure He hears and He cares.

Thankfulness should describe the life of a believer. In every situation, we are to give thanks, not thankful for everything but thankful in everything. First Thessalonians 5:18 reads, "Give thanks in all circumstances; for this is God's will for you in Christ Jesus." Paul unequivocally announces that this is the will of God. Why would God want us to be thankful when negative things are happening all around us? Blessing the name of God in spite of what is going on around us speaks volumes of our trust in God. A heart of thanksgiving portrays a believer's walk with God like nothing else. A thankful believer is a testimony to the world that God is in control of one's life. It is easy to be thankful when all is well but a true thank you breaks forth in the midst of trouble.

With much of the negative information coming at us during appointments, fear can be ignited. When fear is present, thankfulness is hindered. When focusing on the depth of the situation we are facing, complaints come easy. As caregivers, we have to be able to decode the information for the ones we care for. We want our loved ones to remain thankful and not develop an ungrateful heart. When we allow ourselves to become ungrateful, we have opened the door to the enemy. The enemy will use our time of uncertainty and complaining to sow seeds of doubt in our hearts. A heart of doubt and frustration leads to more unhappiness and less gratitude.

As a caregiver, I can tell you there will be some hard days. There will be moments when you wonder if you will be able to make it another day. I cannot promise you sunshine every day but I can promise you that a thankful heart will brighten your day. Thankful people are happier and healthier. Being thankful can improve your sleep and promote a better outlook on life.

I am thankful for everything I have learned along the way. I now understand that this is a journey that my husband and I are both on. The sickness is his journey; he has to walk through that. My role as a caregiver is my voyage that I must navigate. While we can assist, encourage, and pray for each other, we each must trust God as individuals for what we have to endure.

Over the course of the past nine years, there have been times when I felt as if I was watching someone else's life unfold. There were times when it did not seem real. But what I have learned is irreplaceable and I am thankful that God has graced me to be able to share our journey with others. I have learned to find joy in the simple things of life and to be grateful for everyday that I am blessed to be alive and have good health.

Have a gratitude journal and write what you are thankful for. On those days when you feel less thankful, go back and read it. You will feel inspired and encouraged. The journal will remind you of the blessings of God and that will encourage you to continue on another day.

Pray a prayer of thanksgiving to God for blessings past, present, and future. Ask God for His joy to flood your heart today.
Use your accompanying journal to write what you are feeling after you have prayed.

I See You, I Hear You, I Know You

See Me Hear Me Know Me

Heart of the Patient

Written by Scott B. Taylor

It is very easy to follow a recipe when you have been given the exact measurements. Possessing those unique measuring cups, spoons, and bowls makes it quite simple. If you follow the recipe, you know that every time a perfect dish will be served.

> 1 cup of patience
> 2 tablespoons of strength
> 5 cups of evening tears
> A shake of laughter.
> Mix well and bake your temperament on high for 1 hour each day.

If it was only that easy.

Conflict between the patient and the caregiver is inevitable, especially when the patient fights to maintain their independence. Patients wear their independence like a badge of honor. But due to illness the activities of a healthy person begin to slip away. The physical disability: walking, lifting, driving, working in their career, and providing for their family become a thing of the past. The patient begins to experience a form of death.

Swiss psychiatrist Elisabeth Kübler-Ross in her 1969 book, *On Death and Dying*, describes the five stages of death as denial, anger, bargaining, depression and acceptance. Understanding each stage is paramount for the caregiver as their loved one will experience a sense of death due to their inability to be independent. Handing over control of your life to another, even a loved one, can spark animosity. This is especially true when the patient has a long-term chronic, debilitating disease.

At first, the thought that needing a caregiver meant someone to fill my pill tray, cook meals, and provide transportation from one appointment to the next. Although those are duties of a caregiver that is only a small portion of what a caregiver does. You never know what is in a person until they are put to the test. No one asks to be tested. Needing someone to vent on was paramount for me. I needed my caregiver to experience what I was feeling. It was not enough to verbally explain how I was feeling in general. I needed to explain my physical symptoms day by day, hour by hour and I needed to be heard. Because my condition was rare, I felt as though I was on a deserted island and wanted desperately to be rescued or at least that was my hope.

Complaints of pain need to be heard by the caregiver. But I realized that just as important, the caregiver must define a cut-off point and assure the patient that they are aware of new symptoms. Unfortunately, the patient will be selfish, not by choice but due to fear of their unknown future.

The patient depends on their caregiver for so many things. Keeping the other family members informed of any and all medical procedures was something I needed my caregiver to do. Also to explain the side effects of drugs prescribed and to intercede in prayer for me.

Knowing that my children knew what was going on helped to lower my stress level. Truth and details are important when informing the adult children. Children and adult children tend to be optimistic regardless of the patient's condition because they see their parent not a patient. They are waiting for them to "bounce back" from whatever illness they may be experiencing. And yet, the patient needs their caregiver to be the communicator to their children to assure them that God is in control and that their sick and disabled parent understands that and is at peace with that.

Family events still go on in the absence of the sick, so the patient needs their caregiver to attend the event. The children of a sick parent need to understand that they may be called upon at a moment's notice due to a change in the condition of their sick parent.

All financial matters must be communicated to your caregiver. Commitments to your creditors do not stop due to your illness and the creditors are not usually sympathetic to your condition. The bills must still be paid. Therefore, all household as well as legal matters must be addressed in order to relinquish responsibility. The caregiver must work alongside their patient to complete official documentation: Power of Attorney, etc.

As a patient to my caregiver who is also my wife, she and others need to know I am okay with relinquishing my responsibilities. My caregiver, my wife, now handles what I cannot, and I am thankful.

I often wonder if my caregiver realizes the strength I see in her each day. I often wonder if my caregiver knows I am smiling as I awake throughout the night and see her finally sleeping and knowing that she is resting well. I often wonder if my caregiver understands my frustration every time she has to use her physical strength to accomplish a household task once delegated to me.

I often wonder if my caregiver recognizes my appreciation for her patience as she transports me to and from in our vehicle from appointment to appointment. I see her labor of having to pick up my wheelchair and walker which are awkward and heavy. I see her placing them in the back of our vehicle. I see her struggling to get my equipment carefully in and out of the car.

I realize the physical and mental strain of the caregiver is a daily journey. The only way to exercise and keep their body and mind strong and healthy is to trust and rely on God's Word. Therefore, as a patient, I need my caregiver to remember the words of Jesus concerning Apostle Paul's infirmities. Second Corinthians 12:9, "But he said to me, "My grace is sufficient for you, for my power is made perfect in weakness." When my caregiver is without strength, she can look to the Lord.

Finally, it is imperative that a lifetime of learning and experiences of the patient not be dismissed because of their illness. The dignity of the patient must be persevered. Even though the patient may give their caregiver permission to speak for them and manage their care, in granting this permission, the caregiver must be a continuing advocate for the patient and never forget to listen and respect the opinion of the mentally capable patient.

One of the hardest tasks of the caregiver is to allow the patient to express their wants and needs and work alongside the patient in resolving decisions which directly affect their health and well-being. Each patient's level of illness is different and requires different levels of care. What the patient needs from their caregiver is to assist them in seeking out physicians who are truly advocates for their patients. The caregiver must trust their patients if they voice concerns in regards to their relationship with their physician. The caregiver and physician must understand the comfort of the patient always comes first.

There are many couples, during the ceremony of their wedding, who use the following Scripture in the Bible when defining and understanding love. It was read on our wedding day as well.

1 Corinthians 13

If I speak in the tongues of men or of angels, but do not have love, I am only a resounding gong or a clanging cymbal. If I have the gift of prophecy and can fathom all mysteries and all knowledge, and if I have a faith that can move mountains, but do not have love, I am nothing. If I give all I possess to the poor and give over my body to hardship that I may boast, but do not have love, I gain nothing. Love is patient, love is kind. It does not envy, it does not boast, it is not proud. It does not dishonor others, it is not self-seeking, it is not easily angered, it keeps no record of wrongs. Love does not delight in evil but rejoices with the truth. It always protects, always trusts, always hopes, and always perseveres. Love never fails. But where there are prophecies, they will cease; where there are tongues, they will be stilled; where there is knowledge, it will pass away. For we know in part and we prophesy in part, but when completeness comes, what is in part disappears. When I was a child, I talked like a child, I thought like a child, I reasoned like a child. When I became a man, I put the ways of childhood behind me. For now we see only a reflection as in a mirror; then we shall see face to face. Now I know in part; then I shall know fully, even as I am fully known. And now these three remain: faith, hope and love. But the greatest of these is love.

My caregiver understands love. The greatest desire of this patient is for my caregiver to know how much I thank God each day for the heart and love she has shown me as my caregiver. Although my actions do not always display what I am feeling, I feel love and appreciation. My pain often overshadows my true feelings, but even in my height of discomfort, I want my caregiver to know that she is loved and appreciated.

See Me Hear Me Know Me

Epilogue

I have taken our last daughter to graduate school over one thousand miles away from home. Once again, I took the trip alone while my husband had to stay behind because of his illness. Our daughter flew to her new school a week before me due to other responsibilities that I had. I drove up with her things and together we unloaded the car and moved her into what would be home for the next year.

While struggling with the fatigue and stress of doing this and truly wanting to be there with our daughter, there was additional stress with leaving him behind. I knew he wanted to be a part of that moment too as he has missed two years earlier when I took our oldest to graduate school nearly a thousand miles away from home.

Now I was faced once again to leave him behind and count on the generosity of friends and neighbors to check on him while I was away. But just as always our God is faithful, and He provided a community of people to visit and show love to him while I was away. I received daily reports from a host of people while I was away on my road trip.

My time away was not all leisure, but I did manage to have an enjoyable time. A close friend flew out to meet me a few days before I was to return home and helped me drive back to Florida. I am thankful for the kind people who God has placed in my life to assist me during this season of my life whether it be giving, loving, or praying.

I purposefully will myself not to dwell on the negativity of it all but see the grace of God in it all. God has been faithful to provide help when I needed it and for that I am thankful. He provided the finances that were needed for travel and transitioning our daughter into a new school. My lists of blessings far exceed my list of complaints.

So I encourage you caregiver, God has not forgotten you and He does know you, see you and hear you. He will supply whatever you may need as you trust and rely upon Him.

At this current time my husband's condition continues to deteriorate. His pain has become virtually unbearable to him and he lays in bed most of the day. On his last cardiology appointment, the physician thought it was too much to bring him in for checkups and suggested that we only come if there is a problem.

His neurologist ordered Plasmapheresis treatments. This is a cleansing of the blood something similar to kidney dialysis. While I was doubtful that it would help, this seems to be the only treatment that had not been tried. The hope was to help relieve some of his pain. To be honest, I think Scott is at the point where he feels that anything has to be better than the level of pain he is in twenty-four hours a day. The treatments were scheduled for every other day for five treatments every three weeks. After a few months of treatment, he had an unexpected reaction; and the physician decided to halt the plasmapheresis treatments permanently.

As a result of the plasmapheresis being discontinued, the special catheter that had been placed in his left jugular to facilitate the treatments was removed. In many ways, it feels like we are back at square one which can be disheartening for both of us. But I am committed to stand with him still believing that God can restore everything this disease has taken from him.

Epilogue

Dear Caregiver,

I know the road is hard and sometimes it may seem unbearable, but God is greater than whatever needs you may have. I have searched and found solace in His Word and from others He has put in my path to assist me. I am thankful for the counselors, support groups, caregivers' conferences, friends and family that have been there for me.

It helps to have someone to talk to, someone who can just listen. It is helpful to have those who can offer advice and suggestions. It is helpful to have input from others who have experienced what you are going through. No caregiver's journey is the same, but there is a kindred spirit that connects all caregivers. Each of us can honestly say, "I can identify with your experiences."

As a caregiver, you need to be smart and strategic about setting limits on the tasks that you take on. Do not be shy about asking others to pitch in. Hire outside help. Involve other family members and friends. There is support available, be ready to tap into it.

I would plan my time away based on my children's college breaks. It was good for them to spend time with their dad and good for me to get away from their dad. Every caregiver needs time to breathe. When family members help out, then everyone feels like a team in caring for a loved one. My husband has relatives who will call and say, "When is a good time to visit?" I know that means when can you use me? The relationship the caregiver forms with family during this time will become stronger and more lasting, even after the caregiving days are over.

Caring for an aging parent is something that many of us will experience at some point in our lives that is if we have the good fortune to outlive our parents. Because we know this is a part of life's process, many of us start to prepare for it before it comes. Whether it be buying a larger home to accommodate mom or dad or assisting parents in making sure they are saving properly, there is a need to prepare. Some prepare emotionally knowing that the day will come.

Maybe you are caring for a disabled child which carries with it the altering of the dreams you had for your child. The majority of parents want their children to go farther and achieve more than they did in life. When a mom carries her child in her womb, she only has good thoughts and happy dreams for her child. It can be disappointing when the parent becomes a caregiver for a child long after the childhood days are gone.

If you are caring for a spouse, there is the grief of the loss of the dreams that the two of you had of the life you would build together. In my case, I had dreamed of empty nest and what we would do together. My husband's work would often take him on travel and I was never able to accompany him because of the children. I had dreamed that once the girls went to college, I would travel with him scheduling book signings in all of the places we

Epilogue

would go. That dream died with his illness. I was disappointed, what started as an exciting voyage would now be reduced to both of us being home every day.

Also, looking at it from my husband's perspective, I am sure he is more disappointed than I am. Knowing that he will not be able to do the things he desired and feeling that he has disappointed me compounds His feelings of discontent.

Whatever the relationship between you and the one you care for, it is not easy. There are challenges you will face along the way. Some will be more difficult than others. There will be long days and sleepless nights.

The best advice I can offer caregivers is to realize that you are not in it alone. God will bring people into your life that will assist you physically and emotionally. And even in those moments when no one else is there, He is. God will never leave you alone.

Whatever position you find yourself in as a caregiver, it is my prayer that this book has inspired you as you are experiencing the caregiver's journey, or even those in the middle of something that they never thought they would be facing in life.

My hope is that you will gain courage from the Word of God as you read and meditate on Him. I pray that you are blessed richly for the sacrifice you have made to care for your loved one. May the grace of God strengthen you to endure the task at hand. Know that whatever you may have lost in the process,

God will restore. Be blessed caregiver as you fulfill the ministry assignment of caregiving for this season of your life.

Sincerely,

From The Heart of A Caregiver

Resources and References

Support groups are available in most areas. You can find one near you by doing an internet search or contacting your local hospital.
– AARP American Association of Retired Persons
– Center for the Aging
– National Caregiver Support Agency
– National Family Caregiver Support

Kübler-Ross, Elisabeth. *On Death and Dying*. New York: Scribner Classics, 1997. Print.

Venes, Donald, and Clarence Wilbur Taber. *Taber's Cyclopedic Medical Dictionary*. Philadelphia: F.A. Davis, 2013. Print.

Strong, James. *The New Strong's Expanded Exhaustive Concordance of the Bible*. Nashville: Thomas Nelson, 2010. Print.

Tampa Tribune Article discussing my role as a caregiver.
http://www.tbo.com/health/medical-news/illness-takes-toll-on-caregivers-as-well-395391

Tampa Bay Times Article discussing my role as a caregiver.
http://www.tampabay.com/news/health/caregivers-tread-an-exhausting-lonely-path-moffitt-offers-support-april-28/1224565

Radio Interview
http://wusf.usf.edu/d7player/ondemandplayer.php?stream1=85833&Dtype=audio&nID=0&radioThumb=&xml=0&onDemand=#

www.ingramcontent.com/pod-product-compliance
Lightning Source LLC
Chambersburg PA
CBHW070615300426
44113CB00010B/1533